THE SMART PRESENTER

Paul Arinaga & Lars Sudmann

For Katharina, without whom this book, and many other things, would not be there.
--- Lars

For Mom, an amazing writer, leader, contributor and mother, and my greatest role model.
--- Paul

Library of Congress Control Number: 2012914776
ISBN: Hardcover   978-1-4771-5998-9
                Softcover   978-1-4771-5997-2
                eBook   978-1-4771-5999-6

Photos by www.istockphoto.com
PowerPoint ™ is a registered trademark of the Microsoft Corporation

This book was printed in the United States of America.

Rev. date: 04/29/2014

To order additional copies of this book, contact:
Xlibris LLC
0-800-056-3182
www.Xlibrispublishing.co.uk
Orders@Xlibrispublishing.co.uk
516833

Contents

Chapter 7

Interlude: straight from the PowerPoint "Horror Files" 93

Chapter 8

POINT: 'N' is for 'No-nonsense slide design' 103

1 Introduction

Do you like listening to a great speech?

Do you like listening to the average business presentation?

 EXERCISE

Write down how many great business presentations you've seen during your career? What specifically did the speaker do?

_____

_____

_____

If you're like most people in the corporate world, you do like listening to great presentations (everybody does—this is human nature) and you most certainly don't like listening to bad speeches. Unfortunately, according to our polls of business people, the majority of business presentations are mediocre at best and abysmally boring, confusing, and uninspiring at worst. Aside from a few rare superstar speakers like the late Steve Jobs, there just aren't a lot of great business presenters around. In fact, we have yet to find a corporation or organization where the average presentation is actually enjoyable and engaging.

Yet the number of presentations given in a business context is astounding. Most business people give an average of three or four presentations per month. These may be anything from internal status updates to upper management to sales presentations to presentations at conferences.

Some of these presentations are designed simply to inform, while others are designed to persuade. Some involve large financial decisions, such as whether to buy (for a customer) or whether to invest (for senior management). In all cases, the presenter's credibility—and often his or her career—is on the line.

Based on our experience working with hundreds of professionals from Fortune 500 companies, as well as small and medium-sized enterprises (SMEs) across Europe, North America, and Asia, we discovered that most people fit into one of four categories:

» **THE LAYPERSON**
These people spend a lot of time preparing their slides but still manage to give low-impact presentations that put people to sleep. Presentation beginners obviously fall into this category, but unfortunately so do a large number of people with many years of experience.

» **THE PERFECTIONIST**
These people give brilliant presentations but literally spend hours and hours perfecting them. European and World Champion speakers fall into this category, as do many speakers at TED and TEDx events. However, you probably can't afford to invest the same amount of time in preparing your presentation as these people do. It's simply not a sustainable way to prepare and deliver presentations, or to conduct business for that matter.

» **THE QUICK FIXERS**
These people want to present well, but they don't have a lot of time to spend preparing presentations, and hence their presentations often don't have the desired impact. Maybe you know someone who falls into this category? Or maybe you even see such a person when you look into the mirror? Don't worry—you are not alone; this is the most common form of presentation in business life.

» THE SMART PRESENTER

This rare breed creates and delivers high-impact presentations . . . but without a lot of fuss. Instead of slaving away over every bullet point, the Smart Presenter knows what's important and how to quickly put together a winning presentation, leaving plenty of time to reflect on the best approach and to practice.

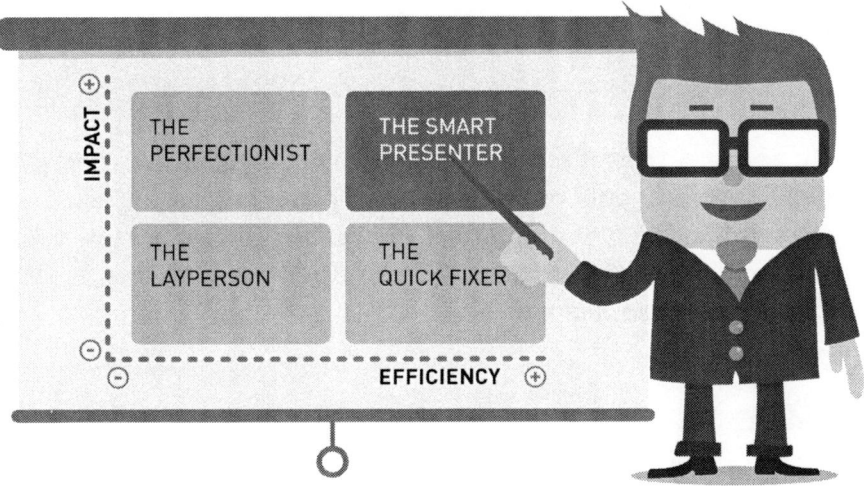

It's not always bad to be a perfectionist. For very important presentations or those that will be delivered multiple times, it may make sense to invest many hours in preparation and practice.

Nonetheless, in our research, we found that the vast majority of people fit into the "Quick Fixers" box. They want to present well and are capable of doing it, but given the volume of presentations they must deliver, plus the other demands of business life, they simply lack the time to prepare properly. If you're giving one presentation a week or even one a month, you probably don't have a lot of time to spend on preparation and practice. In addition, if your presentation is simply a routine status update, maybe you don't even want to invest a lot of time in it.

What is your "Presentation ROI"

The point we want to make with the above discussion and the matrix is that the true effectiveness of presentations should be measured based on return on investment (ROI). And presentation ROI is a function of audience impact divided by time investment.

$$\text{Presentation ROI} \quad \frac{\text{Audience impact}}{\text{Time investment}}$$

In our research, we realized that the majority of organizations and professionals measure only one dimension of presentations: impact. They fail to consider the other important dimension: efficiency. How much time does it take to prepare presentations? And how much time is wasted due to poor presentations?

"... the true effectiveness of presentations should be measured based on return on investment (ROI)."

Moreover, not only can most business people not afford to spend 30 hours per presentation in preparation time, most may be spending time on the wrong activities.

Pareto your next presentation: the 20% that gives 80%

The best way to boost presentation ROI is to leverage the way you prepare and deliver presentations. In 1897, the Italian economist Wilfredo Pareto observed that the distribution of wealth across the population was predictably unbalanced. Put in simple terms, he discovered that 80 percent of results flow from 20 percent of effort. When applied in the business world, the Pareto Principle (also known as the 80/20 Rule or the Principle of Least Effort) delivers impressive results:

» **20% of clients or products provide 80% of profits**
» **20% of salespeople bring in 80% of sales**
» **20% of a software application's features are used 80% of the time**

Sometimes the relationship is even more skewed: 1% of Hollywood blockbuster films, for example, provide 99% of profits.

The Pareto Principle also applies to presentations: you can use the law to increase your efficiency and improve your results. You just need to identify the 20% of activities that give 80% of your results.

Stay tuned: we're going to show you what that magical 20% is!

Lars tames the monster deck

Lars was once asked to give a corporate presentation. The "presentation" had already been prepared, meaning that somebody had already put some PowerPoint slides together. In fact, quite a lot of them: 30 in total for a 45-minute session. Lars quickly assessed the total material, taking out 22 of the 30 slides. He reduced the word count of the remaining 8 slides by 70%.

If this creation principle had been applied from the start, countless hours of tinkering could have been avoided.

The result: compared to other sessions with the "monster deck", Lars' session received the highest audience approval ratings. It proves the point that simplicity gets results.

We call this "the PowerPoint Paradox": cutting the time you spend tinkering with your slides and instead focusing on the activities that really matter will actually boost your impact.

Are you ready to become a "Smart Presenter"?

The Smart Presenter is designed to help you quickly and effortlessly become a Smart Presenter. It reveals the 20 percent of activities that provide 80 percent of results and shows you how to perform these efficiently and with greater effect.

Armed with this knowledge, you'll be able to quickly create presentations, save hundreds of hours of preparation time over the course of the year, and deliver presentations that wow your audience!

How to use this book

We've designed this book to appeal to every type of learning style. It features:

» **THEORY:**
Theory is covered in chapter 2 and chapters 4-9, in which we explain the POINT formula. It's backed up by real-world examples and exercises.

» **JO ANN'S STORY:**
For those who prefer stories, we've also included a story in each chapter on the theory. The story illustrates many of the points raised in the discussion on theory in an entertaining narrative form. It shows how Jo Ann, our presentation heroine, evolves into a Smart Presenter. For that rare breed of businessperson who thinks that stories are too "woo-woo", we also take a typical presentation apart piece by piece and show you the before and after. In chapter 3 you'll see the presentation our heroine Jo Ann made BEFORE applying the POINT formula and in chapter 10 you'll see the presentation she made AFTER applying the POINT formula. We analyze in depth how she improved her presentation by applying POINT.

» **SUPPORTING RESOURCES:**
We provide an array of resources to support you. These include:

The Smart Structure Quick Reference Guide: need ideas for your structure? Just consult this compendium of structure types matched to the type of presentation you're giving.

POINT One-Page Summary: we've conveniently summarized the core POINT principles in just one page.

In the appendix.

» **OTHER RESOURCES:**
We've also made available resources such as the Information Design Checklist and the Checklist for Giving Feedback.

» **ORGANIZATIONAL TIPS:**
An area that is often lacking in most books is "how to apply what you learn within your organization". To address this issue, we've sprinkled tips throughout the book on how you can apply the POINT principles within your working context.

Are you ready to become a Smart Presenter? Go to Chapter 2, "Get to the POINT - A 5-point system for Smart Presenters" to begin your journey!

2 Get to the POINT A 5-point system for Smart Presenters

To help as many people as possible, we've distilled several years of research and experience into a 5-point formula: the POINT system. It neatly summarizes the key steps to conceptualizing, creating and delivering a high impact business presentation…in half the time it would normally take.

» **P** IS FOR POWERFUL OBJECTIVE

Your objective should be your starting point. Not PowerPoint. Use good old-fashioned pen and paper before you even think of touching your keyboard!

» **O** IS FOR ORGANIZATION

The red thread of a presentation is its organization or structure. What is the flow of your presentation; what is your "story"?

» **I** IS FOR INFORMATION DESIGN

What is the best way to get your message across? How can you best structure the information on each slide? And we're not talking about graphic design here!

» **N** IS FOR NO-NONSENSE SLIDE DESIGN

Looks aren't everything, but the visual appearance of your presentation can support the communication of your key messages, as well as make the audience more receptive to what you have to say.

» **T** IS FOR TURNING TO YOU

The final, and potentially the last step. It's you as performer. How do YOU best connect with your audience and communicate your message?

3 Jo Ann's story:
A typical presentation

Before delving into the theory and to set the stage, let's now look at an average presentation in its entirety – one that could be made anywhere in the world.

In the following we will introduce you to Jo Ann, a professional who could be working in any business, public sector organization or non-profit. The situation we present here and throughout the book is fictitious, but based on real life experience.

Jo Ann's presentation, and its evolution, is designed to show you how to apply the POINT principles. It shows you her presentation before applying POINT and after applying POINT. Moreover, we discuss in detail how Jo Ann applies each aspect of the POINT formula.

We will follow Jo Ann and her presentation throughout this book.

=== JO ANN ===
Head of Marketing ACME Inc.

Jo Ann is Head of Marketing at ACME Inc.

She's also visibly nervous. She's desperately fiddling with the data projector connector so that she can show her slides. There's an uncomfortable silence throughout the room. The 10 people gathered in the room, all members of the budget committee, are busy executives and slightly stressed as it's budget review season.

Finally, the projector works and Jo Ann can start her presentation...

What she showed...

And what she said.

- Hi, my name is Jo Ann O Flannagean,
- It is great to have you here
- I will talk about the Marketing Budget Update and Proposal Today

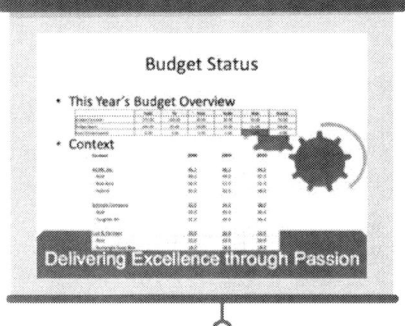

- Here is the budget status.
- All numbers are clear
- In Print we were 4 underspend
- In Radio we were 3 underspend
- In web we were 6 overspend
- In TV, we were 7 underspend
- In total, we were 5 underspend
- This all in the context of changing share status, as per the table

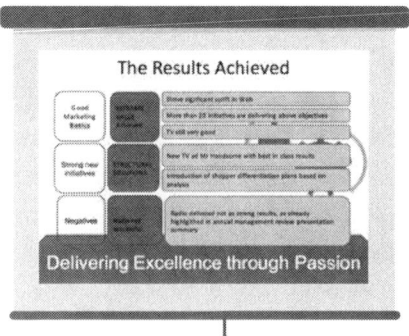

- We achieved a lot of things with this.
- We have achieved a reframing of value.
- TV is still very good
- More than 20 initiatives were above objective
- There were also several strong new initiations.
- We introduced shopper-based differentiation planes based on analysis to bring the impact up
- Radio was not that successful

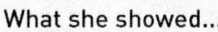 What she showed...

And what she said.

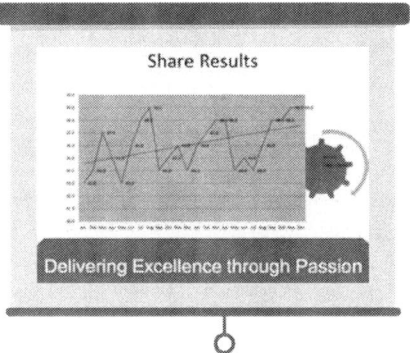

• This all resulted in a share development that went up

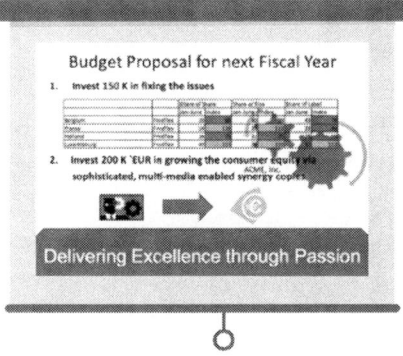

Coming to the next fiscal year, our proposal is to spend 150 K in fixing some of the issues we have seen this year, and continuing other efforts.

On the other hand, we also want to invest 200 K of the budget in growing equity via new synergy copies!

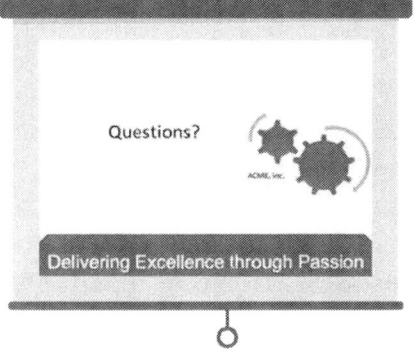

"Do you have any questions...?"

Jo Ann had safely navigated her budget presentation. But she wasn't satisfied. "That was pretty bad..." She thought to herself.

Little did she know that her boss was thinking exactly the same thing!

"Jo Ann really needs to brush up on her presentation skills," her boss thought to herself. "The slides were barely legible and I don't think many people could get what she was trying to say."

Jo Ann was feeling down. All the books she'd read and the presentation training she'd had didn't seem to have helped much.

But life goes on.

The very next day Jo Ann attended the largest conference and trade show in her industry. She was really impressed by the keynote speaker. His presentation was entertaining, informative and easy to follow.

Jo Ann was so impressed that during the coffee break she worked her way through the crowd to strike up a conversation with the presenter.

 "That was a really amazing presentation," she gushed. "It must have taken you days to prepare."

 "Actually, it only took two hours," said the presenter, with a bemused look on his face.

 "You're kidding!" exclaimed Jo Ann.

 "No, I'm totally serious," said the man. "It really only took me two hours to prepare. I keep track of such things."

Jo Ann couldn't believe her ears. She typically spent at least a day preparing her presentations, if not more. Nonetheless, she was intrigued as the man's calm demeanor suggested that maybe he wasn't exaggerating.

"What's your secret?" she asked.

 "Well, how much time do you typically spend making your presentations?" asked the presenter.

 "Maybe about a day," said Jo Ann sheepishly.

 "And what kind of results do you get?" he asked.

 "Results?" Jo Ann looked puzzled.

 "I assume you want to get your audience to agree with you, take a certain action or absorb the information you provide them," said the man. "The point is that most people seem to fall into one of three boxes. There are the ones who spend hours tinkering with their presentations to make them perfect. These kind of presentations get results but at a tremendous cost in terms of time and effort."

 "So, they're perfectionists," said Jo Ann.

 "Exactly," said the presenter.

"At the other end of the scale you have the people who spend hardly any time at all preparing, but it shows up in the results they get…or don't get. I call these types the 'Quick Fixers'," he continued.

"Then there is what I call the 'Lay people'," said the man. "These people spend a lot of time preparing but don't get the results they want."

 "I wonder which category I fit into…?" Jo Ann wondered aloud, wincing.

"There's still another category," said the presenter, with a gleam in his eye. "It's what I call the 'SmartPresenter'. These people create and deliver high impact presentations...but without a lot of fuss."

 "What do you mean?" asked Jo Ann.

 "Well, instead of spending their time tinkering with their presentation, Smart Presenters know what's important and how to quickly put together a great presentation."

 "Ah, so it's about getting the maximum result for the least amount of effort," said Jo Ann.

 *"Exactly, it's what I call '**Presentation ROI**'," said the man.*

The lights flashed, indicating that the coffee break was over.

Not wanting to lose this valuable contact, Jo Ann mustered her courage and asked: "Could we maybe meet for lunch some time? I'd love to pick your brains about presenting."

"Sure," said the man, and they made an appointment for the following week.

 To be continued in Chapter 4, POINT: 'P' is for 'Powerful objective'. Read the chapter and hear about Jo Ann's Powerful Objective.

Go to Chapter 2 for an overview of the POINT formula.

4 POINT: 'P' is for 'Powerful objective'

When you have to prepare a presentation, how do you start? If you're like most people, you probably give a little thought to the purpose and objective, but pretty quickly give in to the temptations of "PowerPoint-itis".

What's "PowerPoint-itis"? It's the temptation to immediately start assembling slides and tinkering with the finer technical details of your presentation, rather than first figuring out what your purpose and objectives are.

Write down a one-sentence objective

When we say "set an objective" we don't mean "have a fuzzy, rough objective in your head". We mean "have a crystal clear objective". And the best way to get your objective crystal clear is to write it down.

Start by asking: "what's the purpose of my presentation?"

Every presentation has general and specific objectives.

There are 4 types of general objectives:

» **TO INFORM**
» **TO PERSUADE**
» **TO ENTERTAIN**
» **TO INSPIRE**

But, of course, you need to be more specific. What is it that you really want to accomplish? What do you want the audience to remember from your presentation? What do you want them to do? What do you want them to think?

You absolutely need to distil your objective down to a single, clear statement. Here's the template:

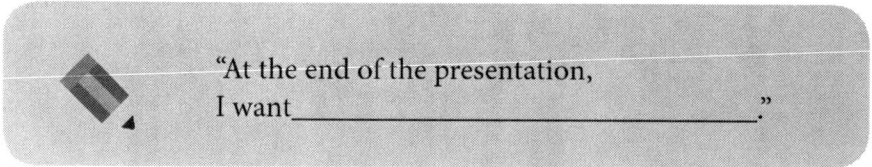

"At the end of the presentation,
I want_____."

Simple but effective.

It should be one, clear sentence. Not a run-on sentence and not a jumbled collection of multiple objectives. Ideally, you should have just one, crystal clear objective and certainly no more than three.
"But I have multiple objectives", you may say. True, but if you really ex-

amine your objectives you may find that one of them is an overriding objective while the others support it or lead to it as part of an overall process of persuasion. Even if you really have multiple objectives, try to stick with no more than three and above all keep it simple!

And remember:
"If it's not written down, it doesn't exist."

Here are some examples:

» **TO INFORM AND PERSUADE**
"At the end of the presentation, I want my audience to understand the marketing activities or campaigns which underperformed and those which out performed so that they approve my proposed budget."

» **TO PERSUADE AND INSPIRE**
"At the end of the presentation, I want people to be convinced that climate change is real and to be motivated to personally take action to mitigate its effects."

» **TO ENTERTAIN**
"At the end of the presentation, I want my audience to have laughed a lot and to feel like they're really part of the team."

WHAT'S YOUR "CALL TO ACTION"?

Another approach or way of looking at this is to ask: "what's my 'call to action'"?

In the world of advertising, ads and direct mail promotions often have what's known as a "call to action". The marketer thinks beforehand what she wants to accomplish with the ad. Does she want merely to create awareness, to inform, or that the audience takes a specific action (e.g. buy the product, register on a website). Similarly, you should consider what your call to action is.

WHY BOTHER?

"Why should I bother writing my objective down, it's all in my head anyway?" you may ask. The reason is simple: writing it down forces you to be crystal clear about what it is that you want to accomplish with your presentation. And being clear about what you want increases the likelihood that you'll actually achieve it. (Do you think Olympic athletes have vague or complex multiple objectives?) Plus, when you're clear about your objective it's easier to find the best way to realize it. For example, with a sales presentation is your objective to make the sale or simply to advance to the next step in the sales process?

One of the biggest reasons for setting a clear objective is to be able to determine whether you've achieved it or not. In other words, how will you know if your presentation was a success? By having a clear objective to measure it against!

 EXERCISE

Think about a presentation that you will have to give in the near or medium-term future. It could be a budget update or a project status update. Any presentation will do.

Now write down your objective for this presentation. Do it now, even if you don't yet know the full details of your presentation.

_____

_____

_____

_____

ORGANIZATIONAL TIP

Before you spend time fleshing out your presentation, why not check your objective with your boss and colleagues? You can avoid a lot of misunderstandings and wasted time with this one simple step. It's another reason why it makes sense to precisely define your objective before you start developing your presentation.

UNDERSTAND YOUR AUDIENCE

Once your objectives are clear, the next step is to understand your audience. You can consider:

» Demographics: Age, income, education, gender, etc.
» Psychographics: Culture, personal style, lifestyle, mentality, fears, aspirations, etc.
» Learning style: Thinking (conceptual), feeling, doing, talking.
» Cognitive type: Analytical, imaginative, sequential, interpersonal.

EXERCISE

Think about a time when you gave a presentation and something came between you and the audience. Were there disturbances? If yes, what happened? Please write down exactly what you saw, heard, and felt.

_____
_____
_____
_____
_____
_____

If you can't find an example from one of your speeches, then think about a time when you were a member of the audience and experienced issues.

BEWARE: WHAT'S THEIR COGNITIVE TYPE?

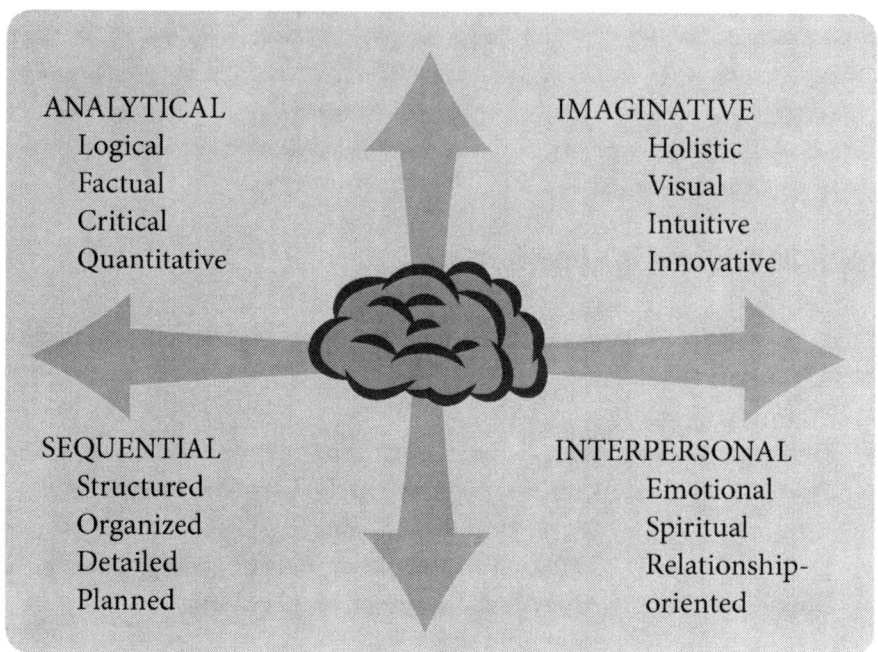

Different cognitive types require different communication styles and respond differently.

Other important factors to consider are:

» **LEVEL OF KNOWLEDGE AND KNOWLEDGE GAP**
how much do they know about the subject and where do they lack knowledge?

» **LEVEL OF INTEREST**
Are they interested in what you have to say? Are they attending the presentation of their own free will or were they obliged to attend? Is it part of their job, professional development or purely extracurricular?

» **EXPECTATIONS**
What do they expect to gain from the presentation? Is it in accordance with your objectives? If their expectations don't match your objectives you obviously have a problem. Fortunately, you can set their expectations well before the presentation (in communications about the presentation, the title of the presentation, etc.) as well as right before you present (depending upon the context and type of presentation, either you yourself can explain what you will present and what your objectives are or you can have the person introducing you make them clear).

» **SOCIAL / POLITICAL**
What is the hierarchical position of the audience? Are they all part of the management team? A mixed audience? What are the power relations between members of the audience? What are the group dynamics? Who are your supporters/allies/benefactors? Who are your followers? Who are your critics/enemies/skeptics? Who is neutral? Who is the "opinion leader" within the group? These points can be particularly important when your objective is to persuade.

» **DECISION MAKING UNIT (DMU)**
Who can make decisions? Who can obstruct decisions? Who can influence decisions?

» **LANGUAGE**

For international audiences, how good is their command of the language in which you will be presenting? If you're presenting in a language that is not their native language and their level is not high, then obviously you'll need to adapt the words and phrases you use, avoid using difficult idiomatic expressions and perhaps even speak more slowly. Be careful also about words that have different meanings: e.g. "pants" are underwear in the UK and trousers in the US.

» **MOOD**

What's the mood of the audience? Is it hostile, friendly or neutral? Will they be trying to find flaws in your arguments or do they want you to succeed?

» **KEY CONCERNS**

Often an audience has a few key concerns. They may be worried that your new product will cannibalize sales of their product, for example. If you acknowledge and address their concerns adequately, you can clear the last hurdle to gaining their full support. It's for this reason that sometimes your biggest critic suddenly becomes your biggest supporter. But you have to know what their key concerns are and act accordingly.

These are a lot of factors to consider, which is why in the marketing and user interface design worlds analysts sometimes create "personas". These are descriptions of a prototypical member of your target audience. You give them a name (and maybe even a photo) and assign attributes to them from some of the categories mentioned above. While this may be more work than is necessary for your presentation, it's probably not a bad idea to at least consider the list above and jot down a few key attributes that would apply to your audience. Just remember that every presentation is different so not all of the categories will apply all of the time.

Ultimately, your purpose in understanding your audience is to be able to determine the best way to reach them. How should you appeal to them?

What words should you use? Should you use statistics or stories or both? How should you structure your presentation? What should you say to them?

 ORGANIZATIONAL TIP:

» *What is the prevailing mood towards you, your organization/ department and your message?*
» *Who are the key individuals within the audience – the opinion leaders – whom you need to reach?*
» *What is the mindset of the members of your audience?*
» *What objections is your audience likely to have and how can you overcome or short-circuit them?*

You don't need to kow-tow to your audience, but it does make sense to tailor your presentation to their needs.

 EXERCISE

Now – armed with the above knowledge and having understood your audience and the context beforehand – could the situation that you described above (p.29) have been avoided? What would you do differently now?

Know your context

Nearly of equal importance to understanding your audience is to understand the context in which you will be presenting. Some very practical issues to consider are the following.

- » Have they eaten lunch?
- » Is it almost time to go home?
- » Have they had a break?
- » Is it morning or afternoon?
- » Is it a formal or relaxed atmosphere?
- » Who is speaking before you (and what will they say)? Who is speaking after you? Are you a "warm-up band", the "main act" or an "equal contender"?
- » How many speakers will have spoken before you?
- » Size of audience
- » Size of venue
- » Format: keynote, roundtable, business meeting, etc.
- » Technology setup

Key messages: take the TV interview test

Setting a clear objective is not enough. You need to decide upon one or a few key messages (not more than 5-7 is always a good rule of thumb) that will accomplish your objective. What is the difference between an objective and a message?

An objective is what you want to accomplish. A message is the idea that you want to implant in the minds of members of your audience in order to accomplish your objective.

A lot of people agonize over trying to figure out what their key messages actually are. Fortunately, if you apply our simple methodology, your key messages will literally "drop out" like boxes coming off a production line.

Are you ready to take the TV interview test?

Imagine that you've given your presentation. Throngs of people are emerging from the conference room. A TV crew from CNN or BBC is waiting just outside the door. The reporter asks members of your audience what they remember from your presentation. The million dollar question is: what would you wish that they answered?

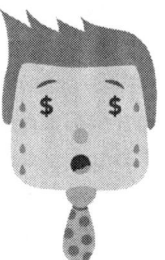

- » A. He was visibly nervous
- » B. He talked about budgets but I'm not sure how it's relevant to me
- » C. Actually, I can't remember...
- » D. He was wearing an ugly necktie

All joking aside, this is what many people answer. They don't remember the key messages from your presentation because the key messages aren't clear. In which case, they may even remember irrelevant details instead.

Learning theory tells us that people – especially if they are not experts in the field – can only recall at most 5-7 key points from your presentation. That's why before your presentation you should think about what these messages are. Think about what you would want the majority of people to answer, if they took a TV interview test.

These are then your key messages. This is a simple but powerful and easy way to quickly work backwards to your key messages. So, make sure you take the TV interview test!

Storyboard your key messages

After you've developed your 3-7 key messages, and before you go into the final organization, you can do an exercise called "storyboarding". Storyboarding is used a lot in advertising and film creation. It's very simple: draw on a piece of paper or use a template to create 6-8 boxes (or use post-its). These boxes represent your story flow. Now take your key messages and write/draw them on the boxes in the order you think makes sense. Don't like it? Just draw another flow or re-arrange your post-its. This simple exercise helps you start brainstorming the structure of your speech and will enable you to find your "story". Once you've finished storyboarding, it's easy to devise an overall organization for your presentation.

A SmartPresenter ensures Smart Alignment within the organization

A good friend and coaching client of Lars', let's call him John, is the head of the finance department of a large multinational. Once, he asked Lars for help with one of his presentations.

 John: "Lars, can you maybe help me with a presentation that I have to give to the board of directors?"

 Lars: "Sure...when do you want to talk? I could do this afternoon for 30 minutes?"

 John: "Oh...no, I haven't done my presentation yet so could we meet next Tuesday or so?"

 Lars: "Hmm...but why not this afternoon?"

 John: "You don't understand – I still have to MAKE the presentation, I am planning to make it over the weekend, so we can only discuss it on Tuesday.

 Lars: "You know what – trust me on this one. Let's meet today, and then we can still meet next week for a second session."

 John: "Ok"

They met in the afternoon for 30 minutes

 Lars: "So, what's the presentation about?"

 John: "Well, it's to the board of directors about a tax issue."

 Lars: "And what do you want to achieve?"

John: "That's a good question...I guess the presentation should be about the tax issue for which we needed the signatures of all board members...I was planning to give a presentation on that, to put it all here in PowerPoint and go through it."

Lars: "So you want to have a decision?"

John: "No, no, the decision was already taken some weeks ago..."

Lars: "Oh...so they all have signed?"

John: "Yes..."

Lars: "Hmm...then is it about giving background information?"

John: "Not sure...we provided them, of course, with the full background, so they have that."

Lars: "To summarize...all information for that decision has been provided, and the decision has already been taken?"

John: "Yes"

Lars: "What is the presentation about then?"

John: "Now that you ask, that's a good question...I'm not sure any more."

Lars: "You know what? It's Friday afternoon now, probably you won't be able to reach the organizer anymore. However, I would recommend that you talk with them first thing on Monday morning about the exact objectives for your session. Be very clear. And do not spend any minute on it this weekend. We can then meet up next week to work on the detailed slides."

John: "Ok, I will do that."

They met again the following Monday afternoon.

Lars: "Hi, did you have a chance to talk to the organizer?

John: "Yes, it was quite funny..."

Lars: "Why?"

John: "Well, it would have been quite a frustrating session if I hadn't asked him...On my question about what the objective is, the board meeting organizer just told me: 'oh, it's just to re-cap the next steps of the decision that was taken two weeks ago – it should be 10 minutes max.'"

Lars: "And what are you planning to do now?"

John: "Well, I guess I will put two slides together – one with key background information and one with next steps – that should fill 10 minutes and meet the objectives."

Lars: "That sounds like a good plan!"

On Friday after the board meeting they had a brief call.

Lars: "How did it go?"

John: "Great! It was very short and exactly what they wanted. I can only imagine what would have happened if I had prepared my full deck. Not only would my weekend have been wasted, I would have also completely bored the board and would have made a fool out of myself. Thanks for pushing for that short session last Friday."

As this slightly humorous – yet sadly typical – real-life story makes clear, it's a good idea to take your objective and the key messages from your presentation and align them with your manager, and/or other key players and stakeholders BEFORE you even touch your presentation software.

Everyone should be crystal clear about the purpose and key messages of your presentation BEFORE you start making slides. Either initiate a 15-minute conference call with key stakeholders or send out an email explaining your ideas regarding the objective to the group. After everyone's input has been received, re-send the final objective(s) to everybody, so that everybody has the document. And once your draft has been developed and you send it out for revision, add the objective(s) you agreed upon to your email as well. If somebody comes back and says: "such and such also has to be integrated", always ask: "How does that fit with the objective(s) we agreed upon?"

These small steps prevent "content creep" and thus can save an enormous amount of time and trouble. Not to mention unnecessary weekend work!

 EXERCISE

For the presentation that you found above, do the TV interview test. What would be the 5 key messages?

IN "POWERFUL OBJECTIVE" YOU LEARNED:

 How to set a clear and precise one-sentence objective. Write it down!

 How to gain a deeper understanding of your audience and the context in which you will present.

 Why you should take the TV interview test to uncover your real key messages.

Case story: Jo Ann's Powerful Objective

It was a bright, sunny day when Jo Ann pulled into the parking lot of the corporation. She had arranged a meeting with the presenter whom she had met at the conference several days before.

 "Thank you for taking the time to meet with me," said Jo Ann.

 "You're very welcome," said the presenter. "So, what can I actually help you with?"

 Jo Ann paused. "Well, I won't give you my whole 'sob story'," she said with a grin, "but I gave a disastrous presentation the day before we met at the conference and I sure don't want that to happen again! I spent hours working on my presentation and still people didn't understand it and nobody was convinced. And I don't think my boss was very pleased either, although she didn't say anything."

The SmartPresenter smiled sympathetically.

 Jo Ann continued. "Something you said about not having to spend a lot of time caught my attention. I was sort of hoping you'd be willing to share your 'secret' with me."

The man laughed and said: "It's not voodoo but sure, I think I can help you. Can you show me your slides?"

Jo Ann showed the SmartPresenter her slides.

 "The best thing would be to run through your whole presentation," said the SmartPresenter, "but since we don't have so much time, can you just walk me through it briefly?"

Jo Ann went through each slide explaining briefly what she had said.

When she had finished, the presenter had an understanding look on his face.

 "What do you think?" asked Jo Ann.

 "That was...really...uh..." the man hesitated to find the right words.

 "How did you approach preparing your presentation," he asked finally, changing the subject.

Jo Ann explained how she had started by looking at all the presentations she had given previously, copy pasted some existing slides into her slide deck, and then added some material that she thought was relevant. "I tried to make it comprehensive," she explained.

 "So, you started immediately to put your slides together?" asked the presenter.

 "Uh...yes, of course," said Jo Ann, looking puzzled.

 "That's what I thought," said the man. "It's a typical mistake. Listen, here's the secret to presentations: 'begin with the end in mind'. In other words, always start with an objective, and write it down. So what was your objective?"

"Um...I guess...I wanted to...well...get the money...and look good in front of the board...and be competent...and give the full background on my complex business..." With this last question Jo Ann was feeling a little flustered. She hadn't been expecting to be asked these kinds of questions. But now she was feeling a little sheepish as she realized that she hadn't really been clear about her objectives.

 "Do you see what the problem was?" asked the presenter. "You were not really clear about your objectives," he said, before Jo Ann could answer.

 "What should I have done then?" asked Jo Ann, feeling a little defensive.

 "As I said, just write it down. Someone once said: 'if it's not written down, it doesn't exist.' I love that quotation because to me, there's no better way to create focus than by writing something down. Next time, just write what I call a 'one sentence objective' down on paper. Here are some examples."

- *My objective is to get my full budget allocation approved.*
- *My objective is to get everyone behind the product launch and to take ownership of their role and tasks.*
- *My objective is to tell entertaining stories about the bride and groom that show who they are and make the audience laugh.*
- *My objective is to convince the legislative assembly to understand the science behind this issue and enact this legislation.*

"Why don't you try writing down your objective?"

Jo Ann wrote her objective down:
"At the end of the presentation, I want to get the 'green light' for next year's budget proposal as well as to have instilled confidence in my team's budgeting and marketing abilities."

She'd gone from looking sheepish to looking inspired. "I see what you mean now," she said. "It's very simple."

 "Yes, simple and obvious," agreed the presenter, "but hardly anyone actually bothers to do it."

 "Right," Jo Ann said, "so now I can start making my slides."

 "No. Patience is a virtue," said the presenter with a grin. "Not yet. The next thing you need to ask yourself is: 'what are my key messages'. Why don't you write those down, too."

Jo Ann wrote down her key messages. At first they didn't come so easily, but eventually she was able to list five.

> » We are good budget managers – this year's budget is on track.
> » ROI's by Advertising channel are very different: TV and Web are the best; radio and print are the worst
> » For next year, we want to maintain a flat budget vs. this year (i.e. no growth) and we want to reorder our priorities.
> » Going forward, priority should be on continuing and refining the 'handsome' TV ad campaign.
> » We want to invest in social media marketing, for example, by introducing a Facebook group

 "Good!" said the presenter. "Now you're ready for the next step."

 "Let me guess," said Jo Ann. "I shouldn't start making my slides yet, right?"

 "You're learning," said the presenter with a mischievous grin on his face.

5 POINT:
'O' is for 'Organize'

When it comes to organization, most people seem to think that "one size fits all". Nothing could be further from the truth. In fact, getting the organization of your presentation right is one of the most important things you need to do to have a high impact.

Why is organization so important?

This seems like an obvious question, but have you ever thought about why organization is so important? There are at least four good reasons why it is.

» **MAKES YOUR PRESENTATION EASIER TO FOLLOW**
This is the one most people think of. When your audience can clearly see your organization then it helps them understand what you're saying.

» **MAKES YOUR PRESENTATION MORE MEMORABLE**
Choose the right organization for your presentation and chances are greater that it will be remembered.

» **MAKES IT EASIER TO BUILD YOUR PRESENTATION**
Once you've decided on a clear organization, all you have to do is fill it in; that's the relatively easy part.

» **MAKES IT EASIER TO REMEMBER WHAT TO SAY**

Paul once evaluated the speech of someone whose speaker's notes consisted of a convoluted mind map (imagine an octopus with 50 tentacles). Since his speech followed the "structure" of the mind map, it was convoluted, too. In contrast, if your organization is clear, it's easier to remember what to say because it flows from the organization. You might not even need notes!

Two paths

There are two approaches to finding a good way to organize your presentation:

» **STORY FLOW**

If you already have a pretty good idea of the organizational structure you'd like to use and/or are the kind of person who likes to "do" rather than "think", then start with the story flow approach. Just dive in and start organizing around your key messages using the story flow methodology. This methodology is a little bit like storyboarding but at a higher level. You start by ordering the key messages you wrote down after taking the TV interview test. At this point, a "story" or "flow" should emerge. Then you can go to a greater level of detail by deciding on the main messages for each slide. Just draw out rectangles using pen and paper (or use post-its) and write down the key messages on each. Under no circumstances should you start using PowerPoint or Keynote. It's best that you do this using pen and paper. Once you have your "story flow" you can peruse the structure section or the **Smart Structure Quick Reference Guide** to check your organization or structure against other possible structures.

» **EMULATE EXAMPLES**

If you have no idea what structure to use or would like to consider different possibilities first, then consult the examples below or the **Smart Structure Quick Reference Guide.** You can quickly get an idea about several possible organizational structures that you could use.

Then you can start to use the story flow methodology to see if your messages fit and flow in the structure or structures you have chosen.

"All roads lead to Rome" as they say. You can start with either the story flow methodology or by emulating examples. Either way you'll end up doing both. It's an iterative process.

Whatever you do, make sure to clearly write down your structure. That's what filmmakers do. Before they start shooting, they think about and develop the entire script.

Beyond a "one size fits all" structure

It's the weirdest thing, but when it comes to PowerPoint presentations, most people seem to slip into a "one size fits all" mode. The typical presentation structure consists of an introduction slide that simply lists all the points the presenter is going to tell you about, the body and a conclusion slide. It's almost as if one took the traditional structure of a non-fiction book, with its table of contents and concluding chapter, and applied it indiscriminately to all PowerPoint presentations.

Structure Types

The reality is that there are many different types of structure. Like a master craftsperson, you need to choose the right one for the job at hand.

Below is a list of common structure types. A word of advice: a really good presentation often blends two or more structure types. For example, you might choose the problem-solution structure for your overall presentation but you could present a chronology of the problem and the unsuccessful attempts to solve it, gradually building up to your particular solution. The sub-structure of the solution part of your presentation might follow a "how to" structure.

The outline of your presentation would look like this:

» **Problem**
  » **The problem**
  » **Chronology of unsuccessful attempts to solve it**
» **Solution**
  » **Why your solution is better**
  » **How to solve the problem in 3 steps**

Here are descriptions of some structure types that are commonly used.

LIST-ORIENTED STRUCTURES

» **How to**

Describe how to do something, how to accomplish a task. Often using a step-wise approach is best (step 1, step 2...step n). Illustrating this with a diagram is often helpful.

» **Lists**

Can be top 10, top 7, top 5, top 3, etc. For example, you could title your presentation: "the top 10 ways to improve your next PowerPoint presentation". You don't need to stick with the word "top" either. You could use "Big" as in: "The 3 big mistakes most foreign companies make when entering the Chinese market". Another common approach is "7 deadly sins" or "the 10 commandments" or "5 things to avoid when...". The list approach works really well because it's easy to follow and remember, both for the audience AND for the speaker. You can also put flesh on the bones of your presentation very rapidly with this particular structure. The list approach has the added advantage of positioning you as an expert.

» **Do's & Don'ts**

This is really a variation of the list approach except that you have two lists: a positive (do's) and a negative (don'ts). This structure is useful for comparison. It can often come at the end of a presentation when you're telling your audience how to implement something. It could be combined with a "how to" structure, for example.

THREE PART STRUCTURES

People are conditioned to think in sets of three as in: father, son and holy ghost; the three musketeers; the three little pigs; three blind mice; and the three Stooges. This is the "rule of three" which suggests that things that come in threes are inherently funnier, more satisfying, or more effective than other numbers of things.

» **Three-Part**

This is one of the simplest, yet most time-tested structures. It is easy to understand because of the rule of three. All stories (or presentations) have a beginning, middle and end.

» **Three-Act**

A three part structure lends itself to the creation of a progression in which tension is created, then built up, and finally released. In storytelling, this is the 3-act structure: set the scene, conflict/challenge, resolution.

» **Promise-Problem-Solution**

This is a variation on the Problem-Solution structure. What's nice about this structure, though, is that you start by painting a picture of the big benefit (e.g. "imagine a world in which…"). Then you use contrast (e.g. "but unfortunately, these problems/obstacles exist"). Finally, you come with the solution, and you show how the solution will not only solve the problem but also create the big benefit that you described at the beginning of your presentation.

» **Situation-Complication-Solution**

In another variation of the Problem-Solution structure you present a situation, then introduce a complication or challenge and finally present a solution. This is actually a common 3-act story structure.

» **Past-Present-Future**

This is a variation on the 3-part structure. You describe what happened in the past leading up to the present, your current situation, then you describe the future. Often you analyze the past (successes and failures) and describe how it has contributed to the current state of affairs, whether positive, negative or neutral, and then describe your vision for the future. This structure can, therefore, be used in both an informative and in a persuasive presentation.

TWO PART STRUCTURES

Duality is a very strong communication concept as in "night and day", "before and after", "pros and cons", "yin and yang", etc. The audience automatically wants to hear the second part in order to have a feeling of closure. Here are some two part structure types.

» **Problem-Solution**

This is a very common structure type that you can apply to many situations. Plus most people intuitively understand this structure so they can immediately grasp where you're going with your presentation.

» **Question-Answer**

The problem-solution structure is, in fact, a sub-type of this structure type. You simply ask a question ("how can we?", "why should we?", "why did they?", "what would happen if") then provide the answer. The brilliant thing here is that you can make the question fit your answer ;-).

» **Before & After**

Another classic one, as in "Before Christ" and "After Death". Some people jokingly use "before event x" and "after event x" in their presentations. This structure type works well for showing contrast.

» **Objective-Proof**

This is an extremely straightforward structure. You start with the call to action or objective: explicitly state what you want the audience to do, think or feel. Then provide the proof or reasoning.

» **Cause & Effect**

This should probably be called Effect & Cause because you often start from the effect or result and then work your way back through the cause or means. For example, "we doubled sales; this is how we did it."

CHRONOLOGICAL

» **Before & After:** See above

» **Cause & Effect:** See above

» **Timeline**

Some types of content really lend themselves to a timeline. Simply state the major events and add comments about each, if relevant. For example, "this is how we developed the first Macintosh computer."

» **Chronological story**

This is chronological like a timeline but in story form rather than as a list of (discrete) events. See "Story" below.

STORY

» **Story**

The story may well be the "mother-of-all-structure-types". Studies have shown that audiences remember stories more than statistics or any other way of presenting information. The most common story structure is chronological but other structures are also possible. You could tell a story using either the Before & After or the Problem-Solution structure, for example. Your story could have 3 acts (see 3-Act structure above) or even 5 acts. You could even use flashbacks, as in films (e.g. "to understand this, we have to go back to 1975 when…"). You could use the Promise-Problem-Solution structure (e.g. Martin Luther King, Jr. had a dream, but…, so he did…").

OTHER

» Spatial

This is usually a chronological story as well. The best example is a journey. It could be a journey of someone through space and time but also a "journey" of an entity (e.g. the fortunes of Napoleon's Grande Armée during the Russian campaign) or a thing (e.g. a widget through an assembly line). It's a great way of describing what happened to something or someone, as well as showing (rather than necessarily telling) the lessons learned or consequences of various choices (e.g. Napoleon's Grande Armée decimated). As people, entities and things move through space and time, they also evolve in their capacities, knowledge, understanding or feelings.

» Comparative

Here you compare and contrast different options or proposals. This can be particularly useful for dissecting strategic options or investment proposals.

» Topical

Main topic plus sub-topics, e.g. communications channels (main topic): social media, internet, press, etc. (sub-topics). Just make sure you don't create a "laundry list" (too many categories can overwhelm and confuse your audience).

» Controversial

If you have to address the opposition or a hostile audience, then you can follow this structure: state your position, acknowledge opposing viewpoints, find common ground or points of agreement, state the benefits of your viewpoint, then end with a call to action.

» Case / Example / Illustration

Perhaps nothing is easier to understand for people than an actual example. This can be combined with a story structure to great effect, especially if you bring in people/characters (human interest). You can also use other structures such as the Problem-Solution (e.g. "Milo had a problem, this is how he solved it").

 EXERCISE

You now have the objective and 5-7 key messages of your presentation.

Using the thoughts on organization, how would you organize this message? What are the options? What is the best alternative?

 ORGANIZATIONAL TIP

A lot of people, and a lot of organizations, apply the same "book" structure (intro w/ table of contents, body, conclusion with "thank you" or "questions?" slide) to all their presentations.

Differentiate your presentation and yourself by using a more appropriate and innovative structure type. People will not only remember your message, they'll also remember you.

Openings and Closings

We've been talking a lot about structure, and it is important. However, ultimately, one could say that a good presentation is simply one that has a beginning, middle, and end. While the structure of your presentation is important, the best way to ensure your presentation success is to grab the audience's attention with a strong opening and leave a lasting impression with a strong close.

"The best way to ensure your presentation success is to grab the audience's attention with a strong opening and leave a lasting impression with a strong close."

Openings

What is an opening? Simply put, it's how you begin your speech. Don't confuse it with an introduction, however. The idea of an opening is not to give a long-winded explanation of what you intend to say during the rest of your presentation. Instead, an opening often, but not always, has four purposes:

» **ATTENTION**
   To grab the audience's attention and get them wanting to know more.

» **ORGANIZATION**
   To clarify the organization or structure of your presentation (e.g. "I'm going to tell you about the past, present and future of computing"), so that the audience feels comfortable and knows where you're going to take them.

» **OBJECTIVE**

To clarify the objective(s) of your presentation so the audience knows what you want.

» **MESSAGE**

To present your main message so it's clear from the start.

Of the above four purposes of an opening, the only one that is a "must" is attention. Obviously, you do need to grab your audience's attention and hold their interest. The other purposes – organization, objective and message – are optional. Sometimes you will prefer to gradually reveal the organization of your presentation rather than explicitly state it up-front (e.g. a story with a twist). And sometimes it's better to let your objective and main message be implicit rather than explicit (for example, to avoid immediate resistance). If your presentation is well crafted and delivered, your audience will soon figure out the presentation's organization, objective and main message. What you put into your opening really depends upon the context and the type of presentation. Is it a fairly routine, straightforward status report or a presentation of the company's strategy that is meant to inspire employees?

What makes for a good opening? There is no magic formula for creating a good opening, but here are some tips:

» **KEEP IT SHORT!**

No one likes a long-winded opening. Your presentation will lose its energy and you may lose the audience's attention before you've even gotten to the body of your presentation.

» **BE SILENT**

Leaving a slight pause after you've been introduced and before you begin your presentation ensures that people will pay more attention the moment you open your mouth.

» **TRY USING STRONG VISUALS**
You don't necessarily need to tell; you can show. Use a strong visual (a picture) that is unusual, symbolizes what you want to say or ties nicely into a story (e.g. a piece of wreckage from a plane crash; "this is what happens when air traffic controllers get confused").

» **LEAVE PLEASANTRIES FOR LATER (OR NEVER)**
A lot of people like to introduce themselves or say something like "thank you for this opportunity to present…" That's fine but if you start your presentation that way, you've already lost the audience. A better way is to start with a "bang" (grab your audience's attention with a real opening) and then after the initial opening say your pleasantries…or leave them out entirely! Do you really need them?

» **TELL A STORY**
Stories make for great openings, provided they're engaging. They can be poignant, humorous, or illustrate a point. Just keep your story short.

» **PRESENT A BIG STATISTIC**
Big round numbers can really get an audience's attention, especially if you contextualize them (e.g. "1 billion, that's enough to circle the globe…" or "20 million dollars, that's enough money to feed x families for a year")

» **A QUOTATION**
People love quotations. Just make sure your quotation is short and snappy, dramatic or even funny (this is nice because you can effectively use someone else's words – e.g. a famous person or someone well-known to your audience – without being a plagiarist).

» **ONE WORD, TWO WORDS (E.G. AN OXYMORON) OR THREE WORDS**
Say the word or words leaving pregnant pauses between each word for dramatic effect.

» **ASK A QUESTION**

Questions are wonderful. Why? Because they automatically get people's attention and you can then position yourself as the "expert" who's going to provide the answer or, if you ask a rhetorical question, get people to automatically answer it in their mind just the way you want them to (don't worry, this is not brainwashing, just clever presenting). One of Lars' training participants opened a presentation by asking: "Who of you needs to fill out expense reports, can I see a show of hands?" (Almost everybody raised his or her hand). Then he asked: "Who of you likes it?" (Nobody raised his or her hand). He continued: "And that's why I want to introduce to you today the new system..." This is, in fact, a classic example of the problem-solution structure in miniature embedded within an opening.

» **USE AN ACRONYM**

People love acronyms, especially when they're funny or funky. Lars, for example, recently opened a presentation with the words: "We live in a VUCA world...do you know what that stands for?...Volatile, Uncertain, Complex, and Ambiguous." Just don't make your acronym too long or complex and consider presenting it in writing on one of your slides (here you can actually use limited animation to good effect).

» **USE A PROP**

Paul once opened a funny story about a cycling misadventure by telling what a beautiful ride it started out as but then suddenly letting the air out of a balloon (imagine the balloon flying around the room) to illustrate the flat tire he suddenly got.

The only rule about openings is: keep it (relatively) short and punchy!

Closings

Your closing or close is just as important as your opening. Have you ever heard of the "recency effect"? Cognitive researchers have found that given a list of items to remember, we will tend to remember the last few things more than those things in the middle. So, obviously, you want to be sure to end with your most important message or messages. There are 1,001 ways to approach closings. Four important rules are:

» **BE BRIEF**
Have you ever sat through a presentation when the presenter simply doesn't want to end? It even gets painful listening to the person. Make your close short and sweet. Then it's more likely to pack some power.

» **BE DEFINITIVE**
Unless you have a specific reason for throwing your audience off balance, your goal should always be to make them feel comfortable. They should know when your speech is ending and your ending shouldn't be so abrupt that it leaves them hanging. When a piece of music ends, it almost never suddenly cuts off. It fades out or has a definitive ending (in fact, the chords also usually resolve). A definitive ending and resolution gives the audience a satisfied feeling of closure. An abrupt ending is awkward.

» **BE POWERFUL**
Close with power. That doesn't necessarily mean shouting or jumping up and down, although such antics can also work depending upon the context. In the ideal case, closing with power means ending by stirring an emotion in the audience. Make them laugh. Make them cry. Make them smile. Make them nod knowingly. Make them empathize. How many times have you heard a brilliant speech or presentation that just fizzles out? All your hard work can go down the drain in the final few minutes or seconds of your presentation.

» **BE CLEAR**
   Your close is where you leave your audience with the most important
   message. What do you want them to remember? Which idea do you
   want to plant in their minds? What's your call to action? It's often
   good if the final sentence you utter is your most important message
   and it may even be good to phrase your final sentence so that the very
   last word encapsulates your main message.

The same tips for openings apply to closings (see above). Two points
to emphasize are: 1) don't say "thank you". Let them hang on your last
word. Or if you absolutely feel that you must say thank you, then at least
leave a substantial pause between your last word and the "thank you";
and 2) always leave a pregnant pause after the last word you utter. Have
you ever been to a music concert where the musicians play with such
virtuosity that the audience is completely captivated and there is a one
or two second pause after they play the last note? That simple pause has
tremendous beauty and energy. Use it!

How to use the Smart Structure Quick Reference Guide

To use the guide, simply refer to the type of presentation you are giving
and then look at the possible type of structure you could use. The reference guide can be found in the appendix.

IN ORGANIZATION YOU LEARNED

 A good structure is essential because for your audience it
makes your presentation more memorable and easier to
follow, for you it makes it easier to build your presentation
and to remember what to say.

How to use the story flow methodology to quickly outline your presentation OR how to emulate examples to quickly find inspiration (see the Smart Structure Quick Reference Guide).

 There's no "one size fits all" structure type. You should choose the right structure for the purpose at hand. You can blend several different structure types within one presentation to great effect.

Case story: Jo Ann gets organized

 "The next step is to determine an appropriate organization or structure for your presentation," said the presenter. "Incidentally, how was the presentation that you gave organized?"

 "Umm...well, I gave some background, some numbers...and an outlook..." said Jo Ann, suddenly realizing again that her approach had been inadequate.

 "You need to be much more structured..." said the presenter.

"Try looking at your key messages, and arranging them in a flow that fits your needs..."

 Jo Ann gave the presenter a quizzical look. "This guy's starting to sound a little 'woo-woo'" she thought to herself.

Despite her reservations, Jo Ann tried to arrange her key messages into the semblance of a structure. She struggled with it, though. "How can something so simple be so difficult to apply?" she wondered.

"Here, let me help you," offered the Smart Presenter. "In your case, the structure was something like:

- *Old budget status*
- *Old budget result*
- *Old budget result*
- *New budget*

In essence, it's a "past-future" organizational structure. Not bad, although perhaps it focuses too much on the past instead of on the result we want to achieve."

"Yes, I see that," said Jo Ann, "but how could I have thought of another structure?"

"Storyboarding," said the SmartPresenter. "Imagine that your presentation is a movie with each slide being a different scene or part of a scene. What would you say? What would happen? What would you want your audience to think? How would you want them to feel? Take your key messages and make a rough outline; see how they fit together slide by slide. It often helps to actually draw the slides out by hand."

"Hmm…this still seems pretty difficult," said Jo Ann. "I think I'd still have ended up with the same structure."

"It could help to be aware of different ways of organizing information or a story," said the SmartPresenter. Some common types are problem-solution where you present a problem and then offer the solution, before and after or chronological. Here," he said, handing Jo Ann a booklet. "This guide lists many of the most common types of structure. You can use it as a source of inspiration. Why don't you leaf through it and make a new structure for your presentation while I make a few calls and send an email."

While the SmartPresenter worked, Jo Ann looked through the guidebook he'd given her and made a storyboard with her key messages. Everything was starting to get clearer to her, even though she hadn't even touched her presentation software yet.

After 10 minutes, Jo Ann had finished. "What do you think of this?" she asked the SmartPresenter.

 "Excellent! Your structure is much clearer now," he said.

 "Thank you. But what should I do next? I can't present slides that are just a bunch of bullet points," said Jo Ann. "When can I start making slides?"

 "I see that your fingers are itching to start making slides," said the SmartPresenter, laughing. "I understand, but there's still more thinking to do. Anyway, first things first, it's time for lunch! Maybe then I can introduce you to my boss. She's a master at information design."

 "What's that? An information designer?" asked Jo Ann, giving the SmartPresenter a quizzical look.

"You'll see in a sec," said the SmartPresenter, picking up the phone to call.

6 POINT: 'I' is for 'Information Design'

In this chapter, we show you different ways that you can present information on a slide. There are many more ways to "say it" than most people realize. By choosing the best way to present your ideas you will both engage your audience and make it easier for them to understand your message.

Better bullets

We've all seen slides like this one:

Integrated Pest Management - the three step pest situation assessment

In a first step we need to analyze info from scouting and pest identification. The second step is the cost benefit analysis, where we need to assess the control cost vs. damage cost. After that, we should in a third step determine the exact need for pest control.

It looks more like a copy/paste from a Word document than a real PowerPoint slide, right? Most people can do better than this, but let's take it as a starting point. How could we improve this slide?

Most people would immediately think of using bullets, as in:

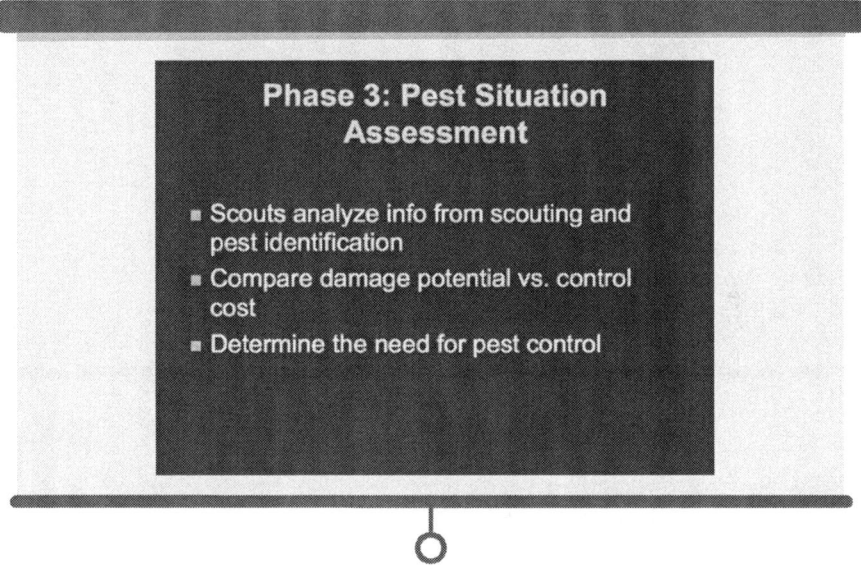

What's the thinking behind this?

The idea, of course, is to reduce the information density and to highlight the key concepts or messages. The typical presenter will try to boil down their message to a few keywords or phrases. One good rule of thumb is: approximately 3 lines per slide, 6 words per line (although, as we'll see, there are really no set rules).

A major problem with most people's slides is that they stop here. You can easily go further and going the extra distance makes all the difference.

How could we improve this slide further?

As a next step, we could condense the information even further.

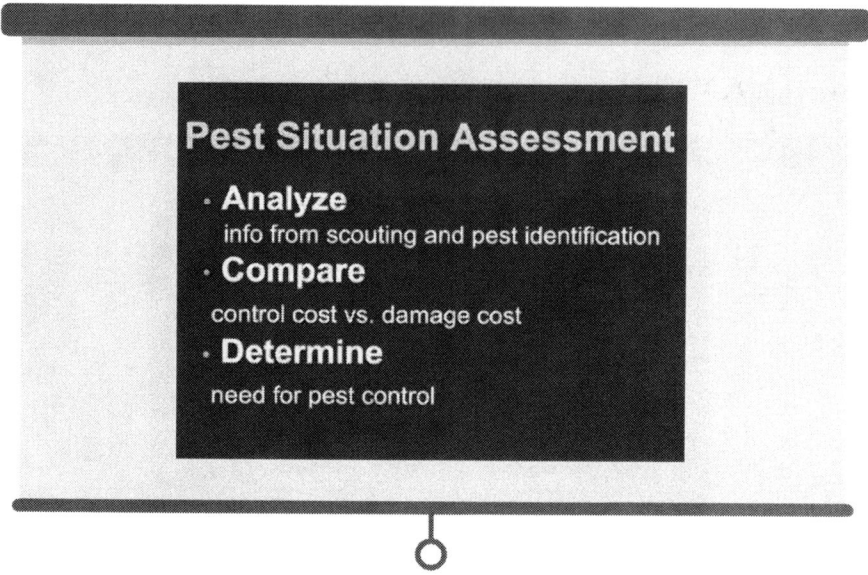

Notice how we **use action verbs** here. We also put these words in bold and in a larger font size.

As you can see, the main actions or sub-steps ("Analyze", "Compare" and "Determine") are now highlighted. This makes it much easier for the audience to understand and remember the main points.

How else could we improve these bullet points? Another approach would be to **ask questions.** Questions are great because they tend to get people's attention more than statements. When we hear a question our mind automatically starts searching for the answer (which, of course, you can kindly furnish!). Questions trigger our thought process and that means we're more likely to remember them.

A question-based slide might look like this:

Slides, Handouts or Teleprompter?

Perhaps to really understand why people make such ineffective slides we need to understand how they use them. We believe that many people use their slides as handouts. That accounts for the high information density of many slides. Other people use their slides as a kind of "teleprompter". They're afraid to forget to say something so they pack it all in on one slide. This explains why many people actually read their slides.

Your slides are really intended to be a visual aid for your audience, not for you!

So, rather than packing them full of information, try a more minimalist approach that really gets your message across. You can use the time you save to practice, practice...and practice a bit more.

SUMMARY OF KEY CONCEPTS "BETTER BULLETS"

- Reduce information density

- Highlight the key concepts or messages

- Rule of thumb: 3 lines per slide, 6 words per line

- Use action verbs

- Apply formatting (bold, font size, etc.) to highlight the key concepts

- Try asking questions

- Use your slides as a visual aid, not as handouts or as a teleprompter

Beyond bullets: 9 advanced formulas

Most presenters limit themselves to using bullets and maybe a few charts, but there are actually far more ways in which they could present the same information.

Some advanced formulas are:

» **Use a step-wise approach**

» **Use a schematic or conceptual framework**

» **Use a chart or table**

» **Use a real or stylized example**

» **Use a quotation**

» **Use a powerful visual**

» **Show a video**

» **Use props**

» **Tell a story**

Step-wise approach

The information in our example really lends itself to a step-wise approach. The beauty of presenting information as steps is that it makes it easy for people to follow and to remember. We're conditioned to learn how to do things as steps. In fact, steps mirror our kinesthetic or physical learning patterns (you learn to hit a tennis ball or swing a golf club as a series of steps or individual movements). Following a step-wise approach, our slide might look like this:

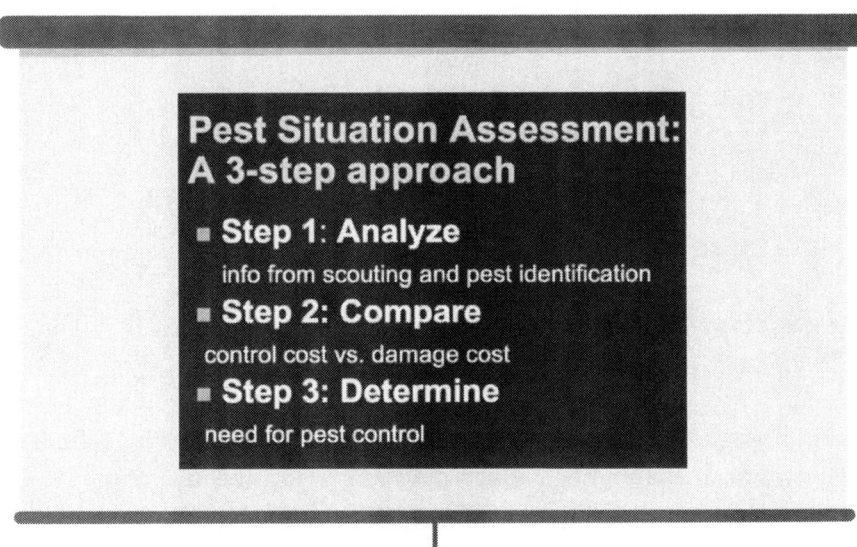

Incidentally, as with the tennis or golf example, breaking something down into steps also makes it seem less daunting to learn.

Use a schematic or conceptual framework

Another approach, depending upon the type of information you wish to present, is to use a schematic diagram or conceptual framework. The variety of diagrams you could use is virtually unlimited (see box). Use one of the known diagram types or invent your own.

PRESENTING WITH PICTURES

There are lots of ways to present with pictures. Here's a list of a few of them:

>> **Fishbone cause and effect diagram**

>> **Input-output diagram**

>> **Decision tree**

>> **Mindmap**

>> **Hierarchical tree/organigram**

>> **Chart**

>> **2x2 matrix**

>> **Positioning map**

Using a simplified diagram is a good way to present our Pest Situation Assessment. It highlights the key decision point: the treatment vs. no treatment options based on a cost-benefit analysis.

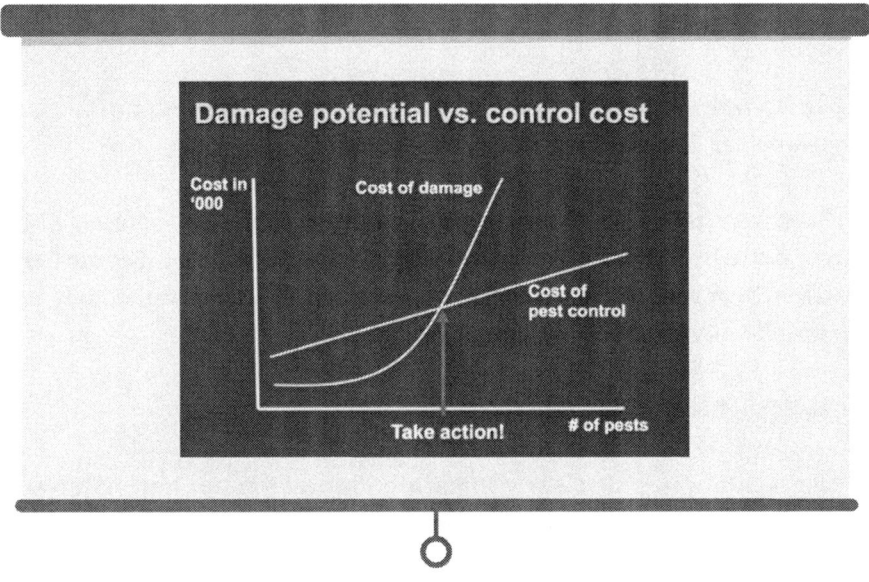

Use a chart or table

The typical businessperson deals with plenty of data and statistics, and performs some degree of quantitative analysis. So, naturally, quantitative information is very often a part of your business presentations. That's why we want to dedicate some special time to this important part of information design.

First things first: some business presentations, like the one from Jo Ann in the case study, are comprised entirely of a smattering of data charts. This is a no-no. Data can be one of the sub-elements of a presentation; it should never be the whole. The full 'story' that you tell counts more than the individual data charts or tables that you use. So, get your charts and tables right, but don't overdo it!

Apart from schematic diagrams, there are essentially two ways to present quantitative information: tables or charts. We will explore both of them.

BETTER TABLES

When it comes to tables, to see what NOT to do, please explore the examples in the "horror files" later in this book.

Perhaps because of horrific examples like these, tables have gotten a bad name. Actually, however, tables can be great elements of a business presentation, provided they are used in moderation, clearly designed and not crammed with too much information.

Some thoughts and tips for tables:

» Use visual cues to clearly separate data elements and guide the reader. For example, use grey shades between different rows; use big fat lines to separate the cells in a table. Whatever you do, don't just 'copy & paste' your table from Excel; design it well beforehand.

» Make totals and other key information bold. Clearly highlight the most important figures. Using bold, applying a bigger font size or underlining them are good options.

» Don't be too detailed. Digit separators exist for a reason; they help the viewer to quickly grasp how many digits the number has and therefore to understand how big or small it is. So, use separators when appropriate. Can you tell easily what this number is: 15465750250? How about now: 15,465,750,250? Much easier, isn't it? But we can do even better by rounding or changing the units, as in: 15,466 (units: millions) or 15.4 (units: billions). A word of caution: in some countries, the comma is used to separate the digits greater than one (i.e. integers) from those less than one (i.e. the fractional or decimal component) while in other countries the period is used (1,500.95 vs. 1.500,95). Be aware of this stylistic difference across cultures so that you don't totally confuse your audience.

Remember, you are presenting key messages, most likely with the objective to obtain a decision, to inform, or to inspire. You are not preparing the financial accounts of the company. Decide on the level of granularity based on what your audience actually needs to know.

So, your table should not look like this:

Budget development

	Year - 4	Year -3	Year -2	Year - 1	Current year	Total
Unit alpha	32543.34	4343.00	5432.00	4354.00	4456.88	51129.22
Unit Beta	54466.00	4343.00	34343.00	23344.00	444.00	116940.00
Unit gamma	5454.00	3434.00	34.00	5454.00	45545.00	59921.00
Total	92463.34	12120.00	39809.00	33152.00	50445.88	227990.22

But more like this:

» BUDGET DEVELOPMENT

in thousand EUR	Year -4	Year -3	Year -2	Year -1	Current Year	Total
Unit alpha	32.5	4.3	5.4	4.4	4.5	51.1
Unit beta	54.5	4.3	34.3	23.3	0.4	116.9
Unit gamma	5.5	3.4	0.0	5.5	45.5	59.9
Total	92.5	12.1	39.8	33.2	50.4	228.0

TABLE OR CHART? DECIDING WHICH TO USE

To avoid overwhelming your audience with data, one rule of thumb is that if you want to present more than 5-7 numbers, a chart usually works better than a table. The human brain simply can't process more information than that in one go, particularly if you're only flashing your slide briefly on the screen. Moreover, perhaps not all the data you're showing is relevant and even if it is, often the trend is more important than the individual data points. Unless you want to take the time to explain the data in each cell, it might be better to use a chart.

When you want to present more complex data, and especially if you want to convey a key message, a chart can be very handy, indeed.

No matter whether you choose to use a chart or a table, we would like to remind you about our fundamental principle for your presentation, and every slide, know the key message you want to convey and decide on it **before** you create your chart.

BETTER CHARTS

The table below gives an overview of the different problems or cases you may encounter in using charts and suggests which type of chart to use to best convey the information.

Problem / Case The key message that you want to convey	Examples	Recommended Chart Type	Chart Examples	Tips
Relationship between two factors	Relationship between price and quantity; Time and effort	Line chart in different variations		
Positioning & analyzing or presenting strategies	Market position (Market growth vs. Market Share, Price vs. Quality); Action strategies	Matrix (2x2 or 3x3) e.g. also with bubbles to show an additional dimension (size, scope)		
Trend & Development	Trend of Volume, Sales, Profit, Price over time; Also to highlight break even or other pivot points	Line chart		You can calculate your data so that base year is 100... and starts at the bottom left... Easy to read; Pivot Point in case you have... clearly show & highlight (e.g. via circle)
List of comparision of relative size	Sales of different business units; performance of departments; Investment success overview	Column & Bar charts; Pie chart		Clustered or stacked; Tip – be careful with pie charts (see separate comments on this); without the right colour-coding and labeling, pie charts often are not self explanatory
Multifactor / Attribute overview	Product attributes; Brand success factors; Project critical success factors; Life Balance factors; Personal attributes	Radar chart		

Here are some tips depending upon the problem or case you encounter:

» **Relationship between two factors:**

To illustrate any type of relationship between two factors, you can use a line chart. The classic example of this case is the supply and demand curves used in economic analysis. These illustrate the relationship between price and quantity. You could also show time vs. effort, cost vs. volume, quality score vs. price, etc. This type of chart is good for explaining optimization issues (e.g. if we increase the volume by 'x' due to economies of scale we'll reduce unit costs by 'y' and make more profit) and pricing strategies (e.g. "if we reduced the price by 'x', we would sell 'y' more units of the product"). Any factor that can be quantified can be shown with a line chart.

» **Positioning and analyzing or presenting strategies:**

The 2x2 matrix is an excellent tool for brainstorming, analyzing or presenting your company's or product's market position. Based on this information, you can decide on the best product positioning and market strategy. The matrix or positioning map will tell you where there are gaps in the market, from where a competitor might challenge you and other useful information. It's up to you to choose what should be on the x and y axes (the important factors). Choosing itself is a useful exercise as it forces you to decide what the competitive drivers are in your market. You can add a third dimension to your chart by using bubbles to represent entities (your product or company and competing products or companies). The bubbles can show the relative size of each entity and suggest how much of the (market) space they occupy. The 2x2 matrix is also excellent for simply categorizing people or entities into groups as we've done in our discussion of the 'Layperson', 'Perfectionist', 'Quick Fixer' and 'SmartPresenter' (see the introduction).

» **Trend and development:**

Professionals often need to show trends or the evolution of a data series. Some common types of data that need to be illustrated are the trend in volume, sales, profit, price or consumption. For this purpose, use a line chart. A line chart can illustrate just one data series to show its evolution or multiple data series to show comparative evolution (just remember not to overload your chart with more than about 3 data series, with 5 as an absolute maximum). The line chart can also be used to show break-even or pivot points. It's then not only the overall trend but the pivot point that is important. You should highlight these points graphically by using arrows, circles, colors and/or labels.

» **Lists comparing relative size:**
Another very common business problem or case is to show the relative size of different entities, either as a snapshot in time or over time. The column chart is appropriate for showing the relative size of two or more data series over time (just remember not to try to show more than about three data series), while the pie or bar chart can be effective for providing a snapshot of relative size (see our discussion of pie charts vs. bar charts below). Bar charts are heavily used by newspapers and magazines, and for a reason – they are very easy to read.

» **Multi-factor/attribute overview:**
Sometimes you need to show the quantity of more than one or two attributes or factors. A radar chart is perfect for this situation. You can use it to illustrate factors or attributes such as product features, brand success factors, critical success factors for projects, life balance factors or personal attributes. With a radar chart, you can show the attributes for just one person or entity, or for multiple persons or entities (again, not more than three, ideally). Your audience can see how much of each attribute each person or entity has and compare across persons or entities.

The above recommendations cover 80% of typical business cases. If you need to go beyond, be careful to avoid information overload.

SPECIAL TIPS FOR DESIGNING INFORMATION WITH CHARTS

Here are some tips for designing your charts:

» **Highlight the most important data element (when appropriate):**
As discussed above, you should highlight the most important data element or elements that you wish to convey. You should highlight these points visually by using arrows, circles, colors and/or labels. You can also give one bar a different color. You can even use a few keywords that sum up the main conclusion that you want viewers to draw from the chart (just use text sparingly; be concise).

» **Data Labeling:**
Highlight clearly your data labels. Add the correct data label to the visual. Combining text (data label) with images (the chart) is very effective.

» **Colors – Avoid relying on them:**
Often there are automatic colors. A big chunk of the population (especially males, and Lars is one of them), however, is color-blind. Especially if you present using a beamer/projector or virtually, colors can look different from what you see on your screen. Then it can be difficult to describe your chart using colors. Also, if your charts get printed, and folks use black & white printers, than your color-coding will not work any more.

» **Insert your key message in short words:**
Guide the reader to the conclusion via the chart as well as the words. Especially when you have one key point (e.g. "here is the break even point), add an arrow, a circle and a short sentence, etc. to guide the listener to that point.

» **Avoid 3D:**
PowerPoint and other presentation software programs offer very fancy 3D chart functions. Don't use them. We have yet to find a 3D chart that adds to the message and helps convey information. 3D skews the visual perspective and therefore only adds a level of 'noise'.

It often only makes it more difficult to interpret the data.

USING CHARTS: A PRACTICAL EXAMPLE

Here's a practical example of using charts. Imagine that we want to present the data shown below. As it is only five data points, we could actually leave it as a table, depending upon the message we want to communicate. But let's see what kind of charts one can create to communicate this data.

Group E	40
Group A	43
Group B	54
Group C	67
Group D	100

3D PIE CHART

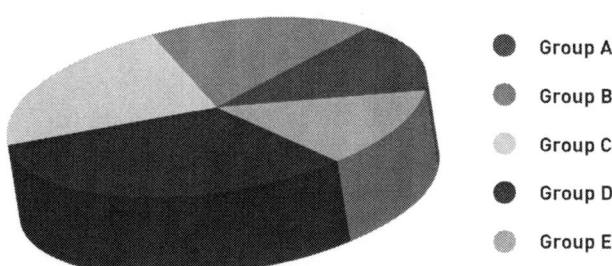

Group A
Group B
Group C
Group D
Group E

A lot of business people might opt for the 3D pie chart. As we mentioned above, however, the 3D actually skews the perspective and thus makes it harder for the human eye to judge the relative sizes of each data element. It tends to exaggerate the size of the pie pieces in the foreground.

2D CHART

Turning the above chart into a 2D chart makes it somewhat easier to gauge the relative size of each slice of the pie, and having data labels helps. It's still not easy to see the size of each data element relative to the others, however.

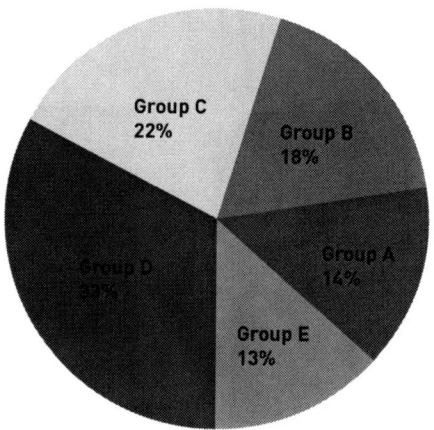

Another way to show the same data is to use a bar chart. A bar chart has several advantages over a pie chart: the data elements are ranked by magnitude and it's easy to highlight one data element (such as Group B).

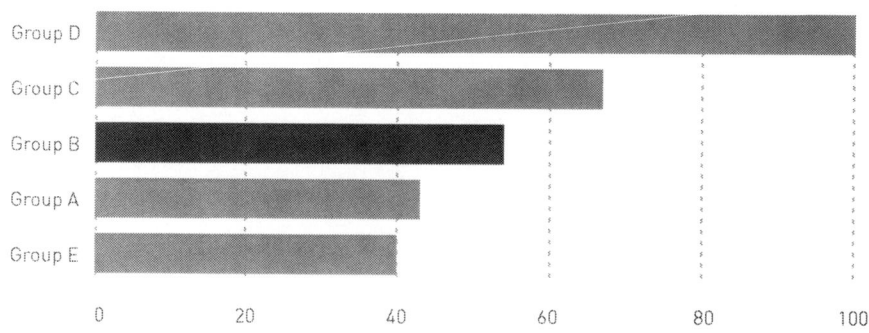

We will show in Jo Ann's case study how to take some elements of data presentation and turn these into powerful charts and tables.

If you want to have a further read, especially on when to decide what to use where, see our suggested further reading.

Use a real or stylized example

Examples are probably one of the best ways to present an idea. Why do you think people often ask: "Could you give me an example?" An idea often doesn't become real for people until they are shown a concrete example of it.

Don't have a real example? No problem. Invent a stylized example (for the sake of integrity, just be clear that it's not an actual case).

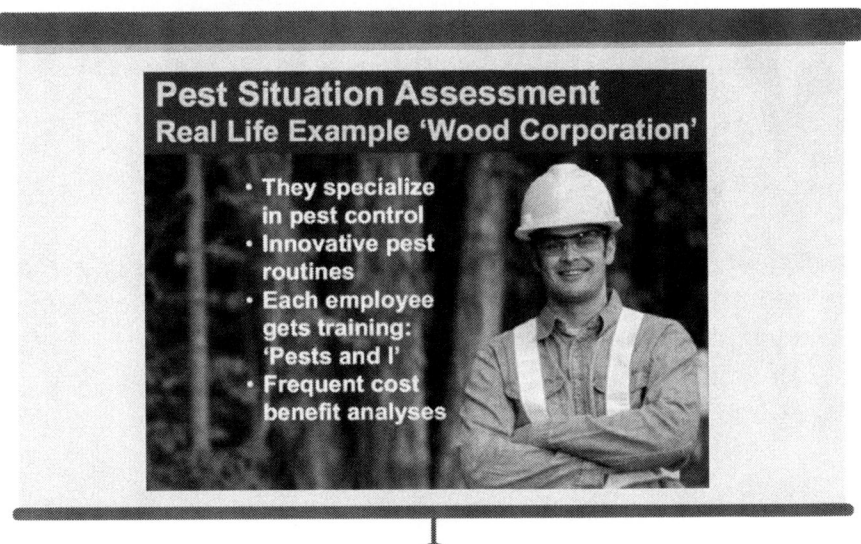

Incorporating our slide with the diagram (see "Use a schematic or conceptual framework", you could show visually the point at which action should be taken (when the cost of damage outweighs the cost of treatment), using either real or sample data. A real case is always better, of course, but don't let the lack of real data stop you from using this method.

Use a quotation or testimonial

A quotation is a very convincing way to communicate your message. Obviously, this gives your message more credibility because it's not coming from you but from someone else. Ideally, it should be from an authoritative, independent source. People are more likely to accept this information as fact than something you tell them (unless you yourself are a "guru").

 **TIP** Can't find a suitable quotation from an authoritative source? The mere act of putting a statement between quotation marks increases its weight in the mind of your audience and catches their attention (just use with integrity, i.e. don't incorrectly attribute).

Another advantage of using a quotation is that it lets you slip in messages more subtly. You can use this technique in combination with other techniques, of course.

> *"Conducting a proper pest situation analysis is essential – especially weighing the damage potential vs the control cost"*
>
> **J. Pesky, author of** *The Integrated Pest Management Field Book*

Use a powerful visual

"A picture paints a thousand words" as they say. Images enter our subconscious mind with little or no screening by our conscious mind. Moreover, when you see an image you just "get it" without having to think a lot. This assumes, of course, that the story behind the image is clear and that the image is compelling enough to capture our imagination. A good image appeals to or activates powerful emotions.

A contrast or before and after approach can often be extremely effective as in our example. It shows what happens when a proper pest situation analysis is not conducted.

Imagine showing a snapshot of pristine woods from June 2011 (the before) and then this snapshot (the after) from June 2012:

It really makes the point well and leaves no room for doubt.

Show a video

A video can be a very powerful addition to your presentation. It changes the pace, and as a presenter you give a third party's 'view' and add another dimension to the presentation.

In addition, video gives you some seconds or minutes during which the spotlight is not on you. You can have some water, look at your notes or just catch your breath.

There are, however, also some pitfalls that can happen when you use videos. One of the biggest potential pitfalls is simply experiencing technical issues (more about this in Chapter 9: POINT: 'T' is for 'Turning to you'). We've had many challenges with video ourselves and seen countless other speakers having trouble getting their videos to start, and then standing there perplexed and perspiring profusely.

Here are our top tips for using video in your presentations.

» **ENSURE CONGRUENCE WITH YOUR MESSAGE**
Above all, only show videos that support the message that you want to communicate. Don't show a 'fun' video just for the sake of fun if it doesn't support your message. As always, first ask yourself: "what is the key point that I want to get across?" Then see if a video can add an additional dimension to your message. Some examples of videos that follow this rule are:

• To illustrate the power of coaching, show an interview with an actual coaching session.

• To illustrate the importance of prevention, show an example of an award-winning fire department that has fully embraced prevention. This example is used by Stephen Covey, the author of The 7 Habits of Highly Effective People and several other books.

• To show what consumers think about your product, show a couple of testimonials from real-life consumers.

Obviously, you always need to ensure that you have the rights for the video that you are showing.

» **RIGHT LENGTH**
What's the right length for a video presentation? It's a judgment call and it partly depends on the length of your overall presentation as well as your audience and the context of your presentation. A good rule of thumb is not too short and not too long. Video clips of just a few seconds usually fail to have much impact. On the other hand, as soon as a video clip passes the 2-3 minute mark, it may begin to detract from your presentation (especially if your entire presentation is only 5 minutes!). Remember: a video is just an interlude to add another dimension. It shouldn't take over your presentation or become a diversion from your main storyline.

» **TEST IT**

We will come back to this point later, but it bears repeating: if you use a video, make sure that you test it well beforehand. Is everything working flawlessly?

» **SMART INTEGRATION**

Try as much as possible to get video files and insert them into your slides. Links to the web are still often prone to upload errors, and the last thing you want is to be fiddling with your technology in front of your audience. Once you have entered the video into your Keynote, PowerPoint or other presentation file, you will have to decide whether it should start automatically or manually. If you're going to show a video, use the full screen; don't show it in a tiny window or on a slide where your logo or template graphics still appear and are a distraction.

» **SOUND – DO YOU NEED IT?**

People tend to think that sound is always necessary. However, a nice moving animation or video without sound (think silent films) that's narrated by you or subtitled can also work well in some contexts. Again, it really depends upon your message and your audience.

» **DON'T LET YOUR VIDEO TAKE OVER**

A final thought: a video should never take over your message. It is still you who presents, so you should always make sure that you add value and extra perspective to what was said and shown in the video. A few possibilities are to start a discussion or give your own perspective.

Also, be careful not to shoot yourself in the foot. A video that is cooler than you might end up stealing your thunder. You want people to remember you and what you had to say, not just your video.

Use props

Remember that we said slides are merely a visual aid? With that in mind, there's absolutely no reason to limit yourself to just your slides. You can also use 'props' in the broadest sense of the word. What do we mean by props? These can be

» **Traditional props**
These are relatively small objects you can hold in your hand; this is what people usually think of as props. If you're giving a talk about Michael Jordan, show a basketball. If you're talking about building a better mousetrap, show a mousetrap, etc. Lars once used two boxes to great effect. To show the impact of packaging size on logistics cost, he showed two packages side by side (the before and after). One was 2.5 times bigger than the other. This made the point very effectively. Moreover, especially for visually-oriented people, it was easier to grasp the point immediately than if Lars had merely shown spreadsheet data. Props have the power to leave lasting images in your audience's mind.

» **Set**
This can be furniture, rugs, lamps or anything else you can think up. Unless you're not allowed to modify the environment in which you'll be presenting, why not make a few small changes to "set the scene" much as is done for film or theater productions. This can help to create a certain mood and transport the audience into the context or setting you want (e.g. a physical place or point in time). It's not always necessary, but could fit with your speech if you need to really get your audience into another dimension, place or time.

» **Costume/wardrobe**
A few simple touches can add a lot to your speech. Your 'costume' can even be an integral part of your presentation or a metaphor for your main message. For an introductory speech he once gave, for example, Paul was dressed in a business suit but at the end of his speech he stripped to reveal a Hawaiian shirt, showing that he's both a "serious" businessperson and a fun-loving guy who grew up in Hawaii. He literally

and metaphorically showed his two sides by using costumes.

Obviously, you need to use props that support your messages. And unless they're part of the backdrop or set, make sure to actually refer to them.

Tell a story

The last advanced technique for communicating your message is to tell a story. This is one of the most natural ways to communicate.

Human beings are primed for storytelling. In fact, before writing existed we told stories, and we still tell stories whether it is in writing or verbally and whether it is about large global issues or our own lives. Perhaps this explains why studies have shown that audiences remember stories more than statistics or any other way of presenting information.

The most common story structure is chronological but other structures are also possible. A story can be combined with a picture for great effect. A story could be told using the before and after pictures in the previous example, for instance, about a community that failed to properly conduct a pest situation analysis. It could be embellished with tales of incompetence, ignorance or greed. Stories appeal to our emotions and allow us to state our points by showing rather than telling – a much more subtle form of communication.

Think about the most gripping stories you've ever heard and they probably included the following elements:

» **An attention-getting opening**

» **A strong close, often with a twist that surprises and delights the audience**

» **Vivid imagery (use metaphors and similes)**

» **Humor and/or drama**

» **Action (something happens, even if it's all within the protagonist's mind or perception)**

» **A clear beginning, middle and end**

» **A protagonist (or "hero" or "heroine", who may be the storyteller)**

» **A conflict or challenge**

» **Resolution of the conflict or challenge**

» **Empathy, the audience identifies with the protagonist**

» **Sometimes personal (stories don't need to be personal, but personal stories or stories told in a personal way are extra powerful)**

The 3-act structure is very common in stories. Essentially it involves:

» **SETTING THE SCENE**
The protagonist is shown in his or her normal environment. Of course, you may also open with the challenge (see #2) in order to grab the audience's attention and then do a "flashback" to establish the scene.

» **THE CHALLENGE**

The protagonist faces a challenge from the antagonist (or decides to take on the antagonist) and goes through a series of trials (overcomes a series of obstacles). The antagonist may be an individual or group of individuals (e.g. the team, the division, disturbing employees), or an organization (e.g. a large corporation or a government), system (e.g. fast-paced business world), culture (e.g. marketing vs. tech culture), or conventions/habits/attitudes (e.g. meeting behavior, short term focus, the power game). The obstacles that the protagonist must overcome are typically both external (aggression, corruption, complexity, competitors, etc.) and internal (the protagonist's fears, ignorance, incompetence, inexperience, poor self-esteem, baggage from the past, etc.).

» **TRIUMPH/RESOLUTION**

The protagonist overcomes the challenge. This triumph/resolution almost (if not always) entails some form of personal growth. The protagonist overcomes his fears, changes his perspective, becomes a better person, etc. In short, the protagonist is transformed and becomes a "new" person.

For further inspiration, just analyze the stories in movies and books. An additional highly recommended resource is The Writer's Journey: Mythic Structure for Writers by Christopher Vogler. The book has inspired many of Hollywood's top screenwriters, directors and producers. It's based in part on Joseph Campbell's book The Hero with a Thousand Faces, which outlines the Hero's Journey, a universal motif of adventure and transformation that runs through virtually all of the world's mythic traditions.

Vogler's and Campbell's respective outlines are shown on the next page.

» **The Writer's Journey**   » **The Hero with a Thousand Faces**

ACT ONE   DEPARTURE, SEPARATION
Ordinary world   World of common day
Call to adventure   Call to adventure
Refusal of the call   Refusal of the call
Meeting with the mentor   Supernatural aid
Crossing the first threshold   Crossing the first threshold
                                   Belly of the whale

                                   DESCENT, INITIATION,
ACT TWO   PENETRATION
Tests, allies, enemies   Road of trials
Approach to the inmost cave   Meeting with the goddess
Ordeal   Woman as temptress
Reward   Atonement with the father
                                   Apotheosis
                                   The ultimate boon

ACT THREE   RETURN
The road back   Refusal of the return
Resurrection   The magic flight
Return with the elixir   Rescue from within
                                   Crossing the threshold
                                   Return
                                   Master of the two worlds
                                   Freedom to live

A word of warning: there is no such thing as a set "formula" so don't follow any outline exactly as is. You still need to use your own imagination to adapt your story to suit your needs and creative vision. Your story doesn't necessarily need to incorporate all the elements listed above.

In a professional context, a story doesn't necessarily have to be quite as dramatic or sexy as a Hollywood story. Here's an example of a simple story about the fictitious leader of an organization, in charge of a forestry company.

I was on vacation in Finland with my family and one day we were walking in a wooded area near the Repovesi National Park.

All of a sudden I noticed something strange. As you can see from these photos I took, the left side of the forest path was totally damaged. It looked like a barren moonscape. The right side, on the other hand, was flourishing. It looked like a veritable Garden of Eden.

A sign on the damaged side of the forest said that it was owned by the "Ignore Ant Corporation" while a sign on the intact right side said it was owned by the "Good Wood Corporation".

Out of curiosity, I asked a worker from the Good Wood Corporation who happened to pass us on the path what had happened and where the striking difference came from.

"Oh, yes," he said, "this is due to the measures against pests that Mr. Good implemented some time ago - you should talk to him."

So I gave Mr. Good a call.

He was obviously proud of his results and willing to share his secret with me, so we met over a coffee in his office. And the COO explained their 3-step pest situation analysis methodology, which you see here. He said that on that basis, they knew when to take action and when not to, and were running a very profitable forestry operation, generating a phenomenal €250 or $330 in operating profit per hectare. He also said that since they'd implemented the new methodology their operating profit per hectare had gone up by 50%!

I'd like to ask your approval to hire a consultant from Good Wood to help us implement a similar program here.

By the way, the next morning, I read in the newspapers that the Ignore Ant Corporation had filed for bankruptcy. The article said that their forest plots had been ravaged by an infestation of mountain pine beetles from North America.

Do you see how this story, based on personal experience, uses a mixture of images, story and statistics to drive home the message? It even includes a little twist at the end just to underline the message.

With its twist, this story is, of course, a relatively extreme example. Your story doesn't need to follow the 'plot' used here or be as dramatic as a Hollywood thriller. It can be fairly straightforward and simple, as long as it engages the audience and communicates your message.

Beyond Bullets Conclusion: use them all!

We've shown you nine advanced formulas for going beyond bullets. No one formula is better than the other. It depends upon the context, your message and the information you want to convey. The best presenters tend to use a combination of different techniques. This holds the attention of your audience much better than using just one technique would. For example, you can start with a story in your opening and end with a story in your close, use a prop with your story, sprinkle in some charts in the middle of your presentation as you describe an actual case and show photos to illustrate your story. Remember: "variety is the spice of life!"

PRACTICAL TOOL: THE INFORMATION DESIGN TEMPLATE

Objective	Key Messages	Submessages supporting the key messages	Information Design

In the previous chapters, you have learned how to distill your objective and key messages.

Now it's time to figure out how to bring the key messages across in the best way.

For example, if one of your key messages is: "The project is on track", examples of information design that can support this are:

» Simply saying the words without showing anything
» Key message written on slide
» Key word from key message written on slide
» Milestone graph
» Table with project plan and green smiley
» Etc.

This is an analysis phase that should take place before actually using PowerPoint.

 EXERCISE:

See these two slides. How else could you bring this information across? What would YOU have done differently?"

IN "BEYOND BULLETS" YOU LEARNED:

· ·

How to apply one of the following advanced formulas, or a combination of them, to get your point across:
- Use a step-wise approach
- Use a schematic or conceptual framework
- Use a chart or table
- Use a real or stylized example
- Use a quotation
- Use a powerful visual
- Show a video
- Use props
- Tell a story

Compared with bullets, the presenter who uses these formulas often benefits from:
- greater impact
- more credibility
- increased acceptance

Case story: Jo Ann architects her information

Jo Ann and the SmartPresenter entered the company cafeteria. A large-framed, imposing looking woman was standing just inside the entrance.

"Jo Ann, I'd like you to meet Nicole," said the SmartPresenter. "Nicole, can you give Jo Ann some tips on information and slide design?"

"Yes, sir!" said Nicole, with mild sarcasm, giving the SmartPresenter a two-fingered boy-scout salute. "Sure, I can help. Anything for a free lunch!"

"Then I'll leave you two," said the SmartPresenter. "Just charge your lunches." The SmartPresenter went off to have lunch with some other colleagues.

 Turning to Jo Ann, Nicole asked: "Do you have your slides with you?" When Jo Ann produced her slides, Nicole paused, then shielding her eyes, and with a mocking grin, she said: "Oh, oh! I'm going blind. This is corporate toxic waste."

 "Thank you...I know" said Jo Ann, turning red. "You are not the first one to say so..."

 "Sorry. It's just that I see this so often..." said Nicole. "But I see you already have a one page storyboard. That's a good start. Now you should see how you want to design your messages."

 "Oh, I left my computer in your boss's office," said Jo Ann. "Shall I go get it so we can start making the slides?"

 "No-o-o, not yet...you PowerPoint junkie." Jo Ann was going to have to get used to Nicole's sense of humor.

"...I mean designing your message," said Nicole. "We need to figure out exactly the right way to convey your key messages. This is still good old pen and paper work. Or spreadsheet analysis work...Or ipad work...or whatever but not yet in PowerPoint."

 "I'm not sure I follow you," said Jo Ann.

 "Show me your first key message."

 "Here it is..."

•We are good budget managers – this year's budget is on track (always tell the truth of course, we assume now that this is the case).

"How would you best convey this?" asked Nicole.

 "Well…maybe like this?" said Jo Ann tentatively.

This year's budget
was on track

	Total	TV	Print	Radio	Web	Events
Budget Foreseen	270	100	30	20	50	70
Budget Spent	264	97	29	19	51	68
Over/(Under) Spend	(6)	(3)	(1)	(1)	1	(2)

 "Yes, that's good," said Nicole tapping her fingers on the table. "But why not just state the key message and have the table as a back-up slide in case people want the details or provide it as a handout to those who want the details. The relevant question is: do they really need to know the details? Does their knowing the details further their understanding or further your cause?"

"That's my long-winded explanation! What you could do is just create a slide with the key message on it," Nicole added, suddenly speaking brusquely.

"It highlights your main message without people having to figure it out for themselves. It's actually dangerous to give detailed figures that aren't particularly relevant or don't support your case. People tend to dive in and start nitpicking."

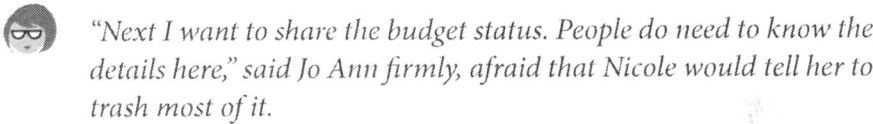

Nicole shifted in her chair. "Ok, good, next," she said, returning to her normal businesslike style.

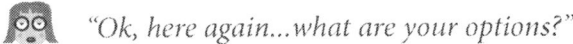 "Next I want to share the budget status. People do need to know the details here," said Jo Ann firmly, afraid that Nicole would tell her to trash most of it.

"Ok, here again...what are your options?"

"Well, I could do a graph maybe...?" said Jo Ann.

Jo Ann and Nicole spent the next 20 minutes brainstorming how to present each key message.

"Now I have it all on paper...what's next?" asked Jo Ann. "I can't just put this into slides can I? It still has to look nice, doesn't it?"

"What do you think comes next?" asked Nicole, with a gleam in her eyes.

"....PowerPoint...?"

"Yes!" said Nicole. "You can finally open up your beloved PowerPoint and start making slides.

This is Jo Ann's final, filled-in Message to Information Design
Template:

Objective	Key Messages	Submessages supporting the key messages	Information Design
"At the end of the presentation, I want to get the 'green light' for next year's budget proposal as well as to have instilled confidence in my team's budgeting and marketing abilities."	"Budgets on track: We have been good and successful budget managers this year"	- Budgets are on track and no overspend over limit	- First: statement of key message; - In addition, for detailed-oriented people: graph or table that shows what the detailed budget looked like.
	"Majority of activities meets ROI objective; however, not all activities are created equal"	- 26 marketing initiatives in total; - 80% above allowed threshold - Some initiatives stand out for good (TV) and bad (radio) results -	- Show graphic representation of all activities, ideally via bar chart; - Show the total and proportion of success; - Add stories of best & worst performer to bring the data to life - Show graphic representation of the total channel analysis
	"Next year: Flat budget vs. this year, but reshuffled according to this year's insights"	- As per guidance, we want to keep the budgets flat; - We want to reshuffle between activity pools, based on insights; - Less radio & fewer events; - More TV and Social Media	- Statement of key message - Chart data visualization of next year vs. this year, showing proportions and impact; - Horizontal bar chart; making key changes in budget allocation clear with support, e.g. arrows
	"We want to continue and expand TV and increase Social Media"	- increase social media investments - continue & increase TV investments - introduce Mrs. handsome	- Show specific and detailed case studies, stories and proposal...go in-depth to bring it to life; supported by pictures
	Can we have your approval for this budget and plan?		- Verbal statement and making the close; handle all discussion points

7 Interlude: straight from the PowerPoint "Horror Files"

Before continuing with the 'N' in the POINT formula, let's take a short and amusing break to see a few examples of the worst – yet fairly common –presentations out there. Relax and enjoy these sad but true examples from the PowerPoint "Horror Files". We'll meet you back in Chapter 8, POINT: 'N' is for 'No-nonsense slide design'.

Why is it that people do not like the average presentation?

Please take a second to think about the average slide that you see every day.

If you want, make a quick sketch of it.

When we ask the question during our seminars, "who likes the average presentation they see at work?", as expected no hands are raised. Yet when we ask who likes to listen to good speakers, naturally all hands go up. We all like listening to good speeches and speakers, but they are, unfortunately, rare.

Aside from the fact that most business presenters don't have much time to prepare and rehearse their presentation, another issue is certainly that many people lack a sense of what good visualization actually is. This can be seen in almost every sample from corporations, large or small, government agencies or any other organization.

Just go on the internet and have a look for yourself. Here's how: type in any subject and add the three letters "ppt" as a second search term. We assure you that, on any given subject, somebody somewhere in the world has created a presentation.

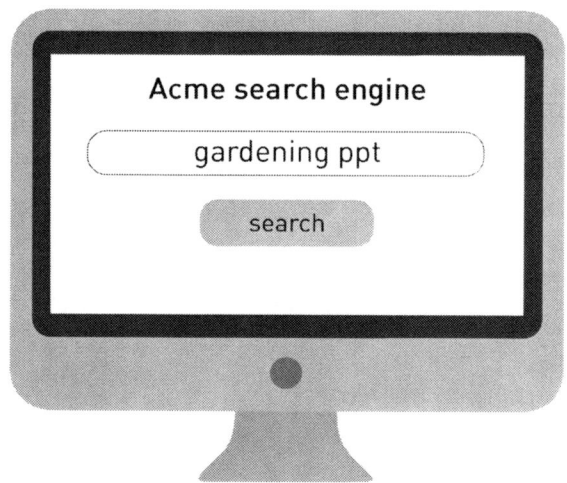

So for example, go and search for:

Gardening…Fishing…District Finances…Pest management (our favorite)…

What you find will astound you! You'll find presentations from gardening conferences and scientists on the best gardening practices like this one:

One of our hobbies is collecting horrible PowerPoints and building our library of "PowerPoints from Hell" that we call the PowerPoint Horror Files. Another of our hobbies is to play "Powerpoint Karaoke" with these slides . . . Just collect a few friends on a nice weekend evening, lock the doors, and have everybody present in five minutes one of the horrific presentations that you find on the net. This can be great fun (OK, we are pretty into this subject).

Like scientists, we have started to create a typology of horrible Power-Point presentations, i.e., to bring system and order to the horror. In general, we see seven types of horrific business slides being used. As the saying goes, "read it, and weep."

» The "Classic": A bullet point monster
» The Quickie or "Let's do a quick copy and paste from Word"
» The "Table Beast" or "I need binoculars in row 1"
» The "Confusing Business Slide...."
» The "Incomprehensible chart"
» The "I am not a designer but I love Word Art slide"
» The "Do you think I'm sexy? Uh, no, not really" slide

The Classic: "The Bullet Point Monster"

Here's a classic:

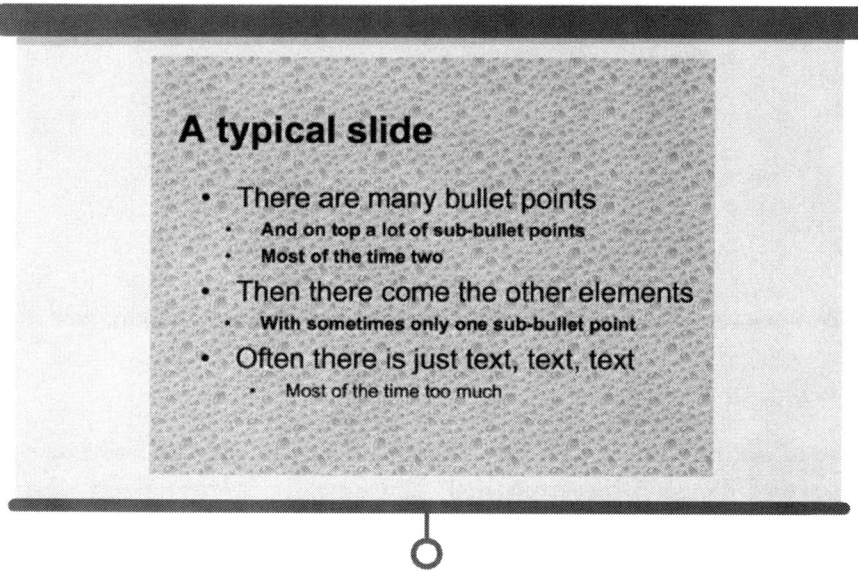

This slide is shooting off more bullets than a machine gun! Bullets are meant to summarize information, not to regurgitate it in the form of "visual diarrhea".

And because it's so nice, here's a second one...

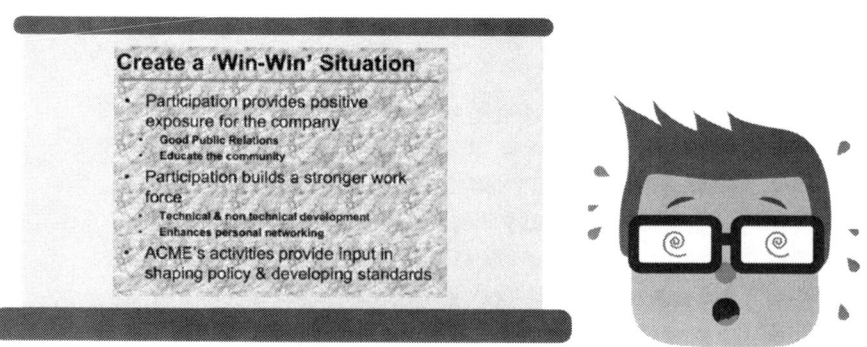

Generally speaking, three bullets per slide is preferable, and five bullets per slide is an absolute maximum. Moreover, do you really need to use sub-bullets? As we've said before, slides that are jam-packed with text are more of a "crutch" or "teleprompter" for the speaker than a real visual aid for the audience. If you really need to communicate all this information then consider breaking it up into smaller chunks.

The Quickie or "Let's do a quick copy & paste from Word"

> ### Integrated Pest Management - the three step pest situation assessment
>
> In a first step we need to analyze info from scouting and pest identification. The second step is the cost benefit analysis, where we need to assess the control cost vs. damage cost. After that, we should in a third step determine the exact need for pest control.

Doing a copy & paste from Word is really the ultimate example of laziness and sloppy slide design. The only time it was every advantageous for the audience was when Paul was following lectures in French (i.e. not his native language) and he could easily follow them by literally reading the densely packed slides. But then, of course, what's the point in listening to a speaker when you can just read their slides?

The Table Beast or "I need binoculars in row 1 "

AGENT	POLLEN & FLOWER CHARACTERISTICS	ENDUCER/ ENTICEMENT	OTHER
Wind	Abundant, smooth, small pollen grains Dull colored flowers, small or absent petals, sexes often separate; well-exposed stamens and stigmas	None	More common in temperate regions than tropical
Beetles	Large flowers borne singly, or small and aggregated into inflorescence, white or dull color, strong odor (spicy, fruity or fetid, not sweet)	May secrete nectar, or the petals or specialized food bodies eaten directly	
Bees and other Hymenoptera	Showy, bright petal of yellow or blue color; nectarines at base of corolla tube	Nectar, pollen, sexual trickery	Bees are most common pollinator worldwide.
Birds	Red and yellow, low odor; flower shape restricts access to nectar to appropriate animals only	Heavy nectar loads	
Butterflies	Similar to bee flowers, may include reds	Nectar	
Moths	Night flowering, heavy sweet fragrance, white or pale color	Nectar	
Bats	Large, strong flowers, dull colored, night opening, strong fermenting/fruit-like odors; Copious nectar	Many bats eat pollen; pollen from bat-pollinated species tends to by high in protein compared to insect-pollinated plants.	

Another wonderful classic. It's frequently just a copy & paste of an Excel sheet. So, yet another example of extreme laziness. Usually when people include so much densely packed information one of three things happens: 1) the audience gets completely lost and doesn't pay much attention; 2) a prickly member of the audience finds a relatively unimportant detail in your massive table to nit pick about; or 3) the audience only takes note of the one point that the speaker emphasizes amongst the mass of information…but if that's the case, then why include all the other information in the first place? Do yourself a favor: only include what's absolutely necessary to make your point.

The "Confusing Business Slide...."

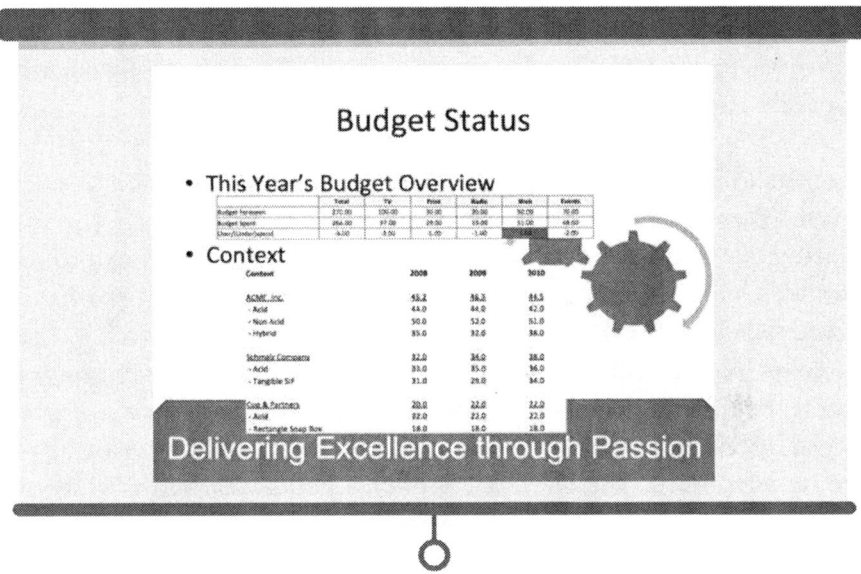

This slide makes us nauseous and claustrophobic. At first glance it seems as though it could be split into 4-5 slides or boiled down to one or two.

The confusing business slide is often accompanied by his good friend and brother:

The "incomprehensible chart"

There are many chart styles (e.g. bar, column, pie, line) and you should

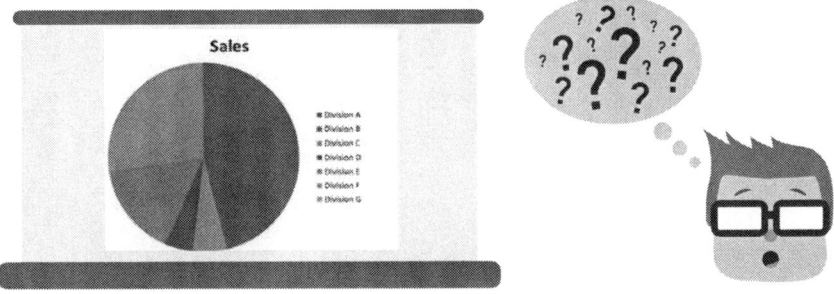

make sure to use the chart style that is most appropriate to the type of data you are visualizing (see "6. POINT: 'I' is for 'Information Design'" for more information on using charts). Moreover, it's generally better not to attempt to illustrate more than one or two points or one or two trends with your data. Otherwise, you risk confusing your audience with an overly complex chart.

Take the Pie Chart, for example, it's one of the most common business charts. They are ok when presenting a small number of data points. When you exceed 3-4 data points, however, it becomes difficult to discern which data point corresponds to the legend (assuming you have a legend; labels could work better). Moreover, some people, such as Lars, are color-blind and thus cannot even link the legend to the elements of the pie. By the way, when the relative magnitudes of your data points are similar, it's also often difficult to discern which slices of the pie are bigger and by how much. The bar chart is often a better alternative to the pie chart (see "6. POINT: 'I' is for 'Information Design'" for more information on using charts).

This brings us to another area – many people know that their material (like the slides we had before) is extremely boring. That is why they try to spice it up, for example with:

The "I am not a designer but I love Word Art" slide

Overusing Word Art is really passé!

And by the way, the question slide is one of the most unnecessary slides that there is.

To be sure, we're not saying that you should not design beautiful slides. On the contrary, we will cover this subject in depth in Chapter 8 "No-nonsense slide design". And it will be of great benefit for you to learn some of basic design principles. There are also some fantastic further resources on this topic such as the classic: Presentation Zen Design.

The key, however, is not to give in to the temptation to engage in cheap, cheesy design. It's here that we again encounter the "PowerPoint Paradox": just because a feature is available in PowerPoint doesn't mean that you have to use it.

There's a refinement of the above type of business slide. We call it:

The "Do you think I'm sexy. Uh, no, I don't" slide

In a desperate attempt to be "sexy" the unseasoned PowerPoint presenter heaps clipart or other pictures onto his presentation, instead of first considering how best to express his message.

A picture says a thousand words… but there is an important caveat to this: not every picture says those 1,000 words…some may say only 100. Some may say only 10…and some pictures say nothing at all. Plus you don't need 1,000 pictures to say 1,000 words.

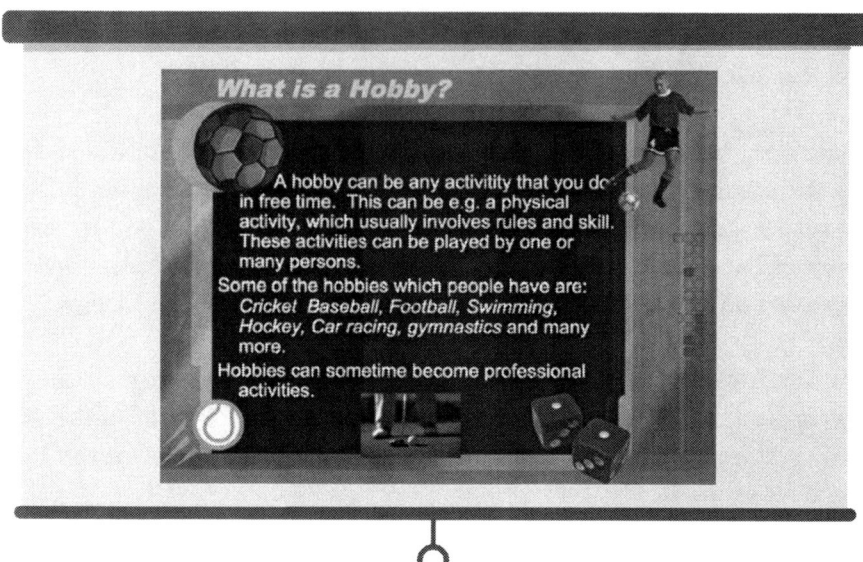

 EXERCISE

Go through one of your old presentations (ideally from more than 1 year ago) and see if your slides match any of the descriptions from the above typology. Try to find at least 3 example slides (we are sure you will find some).

Would you do something differently today? If yes, what?

8 POINT:
'N' is for 'No-nonsense slide design'

So, you're not a graphic designer but you want to have slides that are visually appealing and clear. What should you do?

- Hire a professional graphic designer
- Use a clunky template
- Try to do it yourself
- Give up and accept the fact that your slides will look horrible
- None of the above

You **don't** have to be a graphic designer or hire one in order to have slides that look nice. As with the rest of the POINT program, the first step is to THINK. Think first how slide design – and visuals – can support your message.

An example of poor design

Here's an example of a slide we found and included in our "PowerPoint Horror Files".

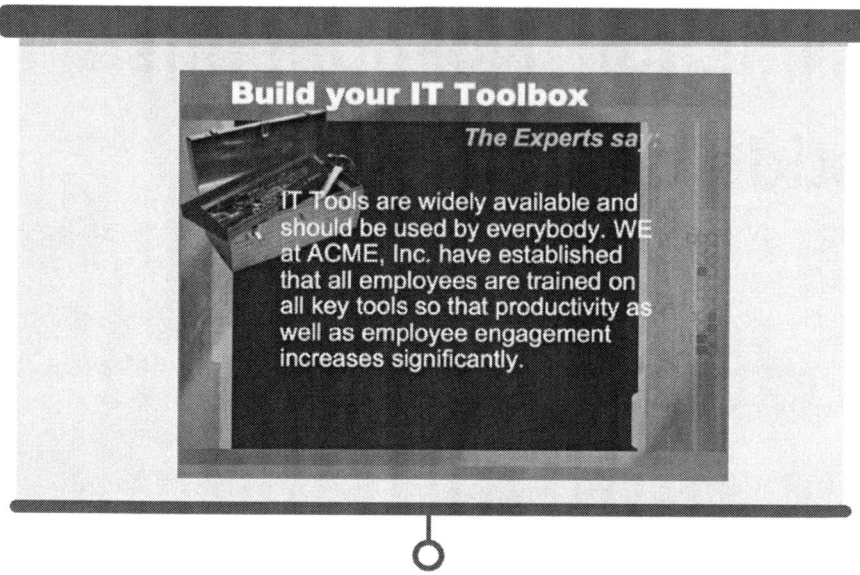

A lot can be said about this slide. To start with, it looks like a slide from the late 1990s. It's also a nice example of a template that wastes valuable slide real estate (see below). Moreover, what do the squares at the very right symbolize? They add nothing to the presentation. There's also a large amount of text to read that could probably be visualized differently.

All of the above are true, but there is one element that we want to point out that is particularly distracting.

It's "carefully planted" text overlap

This is an obvious one, and yet how many times have you seen it? Very often, probably. Avoiding text overlap is a quick win; avoiding this small but significant design flaw will improve the appearance of your slides substantially.

Do you value your "real estate"?

When an artist paints a picture, he or she first thinks of his or her canvass. How much space is there to work in? The same is true with slides.

Do you use a corporate template for all of your presentations?

And does it look something like this?

The problem with the typical corporate template is that it wastes valuable slide "real estate". Real estate is a term borrowed from user interface design. It means the space available on your slide. Most corporate templates have a logo, a header and a footer. By the time all these bits of information or graphics have been included on your slide master, you may be left with only 50% of your original real estate. That means you only have half the space to communicate your message.

> **TIP** Dare to ditch from time to time the corporate design. If and when appropriate, you can even use 100% of the slide real estate.

THIS SHOULD BE
YOUR
REAL ESTATE.

Many successful presenters now even use full-screen pictures to make their points. As they say, a picture paints a thousand words.

Maximizing your slide "real estate" the Pecha Kucha way

A radical new presentation format is sweeping the world. It's called "Pecha Kucha". Pecha Kucha is an evening of presentations using a format that is based on a simple idea:

 20 IMAGES X 20 SECONDS

Each image is on screen for only 20 seconds. It's a format that makes presentations concise, and keeps things moving at a rapid pace. Each speaker has 6 minutes 40 seconds. Although the use of bullet points is not prohibited, slides are typically full-screen pictures.

 LARS DOES PECHAKUCHA

When preparing his PechaKucha presentation in front of 400 people in Aachen in 2011, Lars was forced to put a 40 min. presentation into the compact and disciplined 6 min. 40 second PechaKucha format. Focusing on the visual effect and selecting the pictures – forced him to be crystal clear about he wanted to say and to support it with great visuals.

To see Lars' PechaKucha presentation, visit www.lars-sudmann.com and search in the videos section.

 HOW PECHAKUCHA BEGAN

PechaKucha was devised in Tokyo in February 2003 as an event for young designers to meet, network, and show their work in public. It has turned into a massive celebration, with events happening in hundreds of cities around the world, inspiring creatives worldwide. It draws its name from the Japanese term for the sound of "chit chat".

For more information about PechaKucha please visit: http://www.pecha-kucha.org/.

Black is beautiful

Ultimately, slides are only a visual aid. So, you should constantly ask yourself: "Do my slides support my message?"

 **Tip: Turn it off!**
Occasionally, you can use a black screen to get your audience's attention and really connect with them. Use it when you want to underline a specific point or form an emotional connection with your audience. They'll focus on you, the speaker, rather than on your slides.

How do you black out the screen? The easiest way is to use a remote control device. See Chapter 9, "POINT: 'T' is for 'Turning to you'" for details.

Another easy way is to simply include a black slide in your presentation:

Simply turn the background of the slide to pitch black or alternatively insert a big, black box.

This is a fantastic feature to add to your presentation, as it creates a natural break and surprises the audience. We have become so used to always seeing slides on the screen while somebody speaks. By employing this technique you will be the refreshing surprise.

TEN no-nonsense design principles

» **START WITH THE CONCEPT**
When they come up with an ad, advertising agencies don't immediately start creating images or copy (text). First, they think about the concept. What do we want to express and how could we best express it? Could we use metaphors? Could we use juxtaposition? What is the main message for this slide?

» **LESS IS MORE**
Remember what we said about information density? Your goal should be to eliminate "noise" or extraneous information so that your audience focuses on you and your key message rather than on reading your slides. You only need to use keywords or phrases. A good rule is: cut and then cut again.

» **USE IMAGES**
A picture paints a thousand words. When a person sees an image, they often "get" what you're trying to say in one glance. There's no need for explanation. They just get it. Moreover, they may "get it" at a deep subliminal level. Images can create a powerful emotional connection with your audience. Even if you're presenting a dry subject, appealing both to reason and emotion is the most effective strategy. Why? Because even supposedly "rational" people are still driven to some degree by their emotions. That's what it means to be human.

» **CHOOSE THE RIGHT WORDS**
Use colorful words and metaphors to make your points. "Product x is our cash cow" is much more expressive and easy to remember than "Product x is generating cash for us." A metaphor paints a powerful image in the minds of members of your audience (and using an image to illustrate your metaphor is even more powerful).

» **MAKE SURE THAT WORDS AND VISUALS WORK TOGETHER**
The text (if any) on your slides should work with the visuals (if any) to communicate your main message. There should be no contradiction or ambiguity. You wouldn't say "Product x is our cash cow" and then show a picture of a goat or a slot machine, would you? This is known as a mixed metaphor.

» **BREAK THE "RULES"**
There's no rule that says that you have to use the default fonts or keep all text centered.

» **STYLE**
Decide upon a style in terms of layout, fonts, colors and tone of voice and then keep it consistent; only consciously break the stylistic rules when you want to make a point.

» **MAKE THEM HUGE**
There's no reason why you can't make fonts HUGE. You don't need to only rely on bold. Especially when you follow a minimalist approach, there will be more space on each slide to make fonts larger. See the example from our 5-minute challenge.

» **LIMIT YOURSELF TO A MAXIMUM OF 3-4 COLORS THAT GO WELL TOGETHER**
Professional graphic designers typically establish a color palette. A color palette is the colors that will be used (e.g. for a website, brochure, etc.). It also may identify when and where they will be used (e.g. blue for headings, purple for body text). There's no need to get

complicated here. Just make sure that you are consistent in your use of color, that you choose colors that look good together (i.e. don't clash) and that you limit yourself to a maximum of about 3-4 colors.

» **USE ANIMATION SPARINGLY**
PowerPoint is packed with sophisticated features for animation. And animation can be highly effective. When you want to make your slide more dynamic or call attention to a specific element on your slide, then animation can be a good choice. But it should be used sparingly. Also be careful that your animation doesn't require too many clicks that don't add value and that it doesn't take too much time to appear on screen.

Take the 5 minute challenge

You can take any slide and within 5 minutes transform it into something that's clear, elegant and beautiful by applying our TEN no-nonsense design principles and using your common sense. We applied our design principles to the slide below, for example. It's already a very nice slide, but could be improved further.

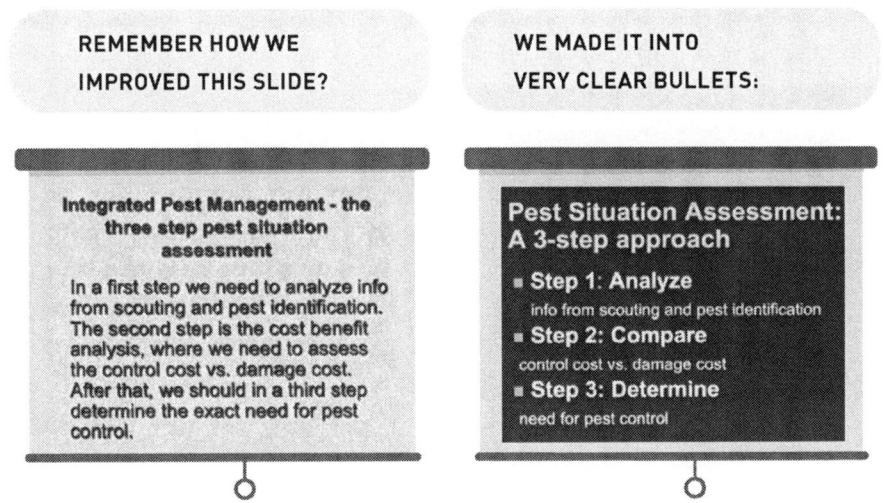

The slide above is already a major improvement. But we realized that we could do even better. So, we took the "five minute challenge". And here's the result

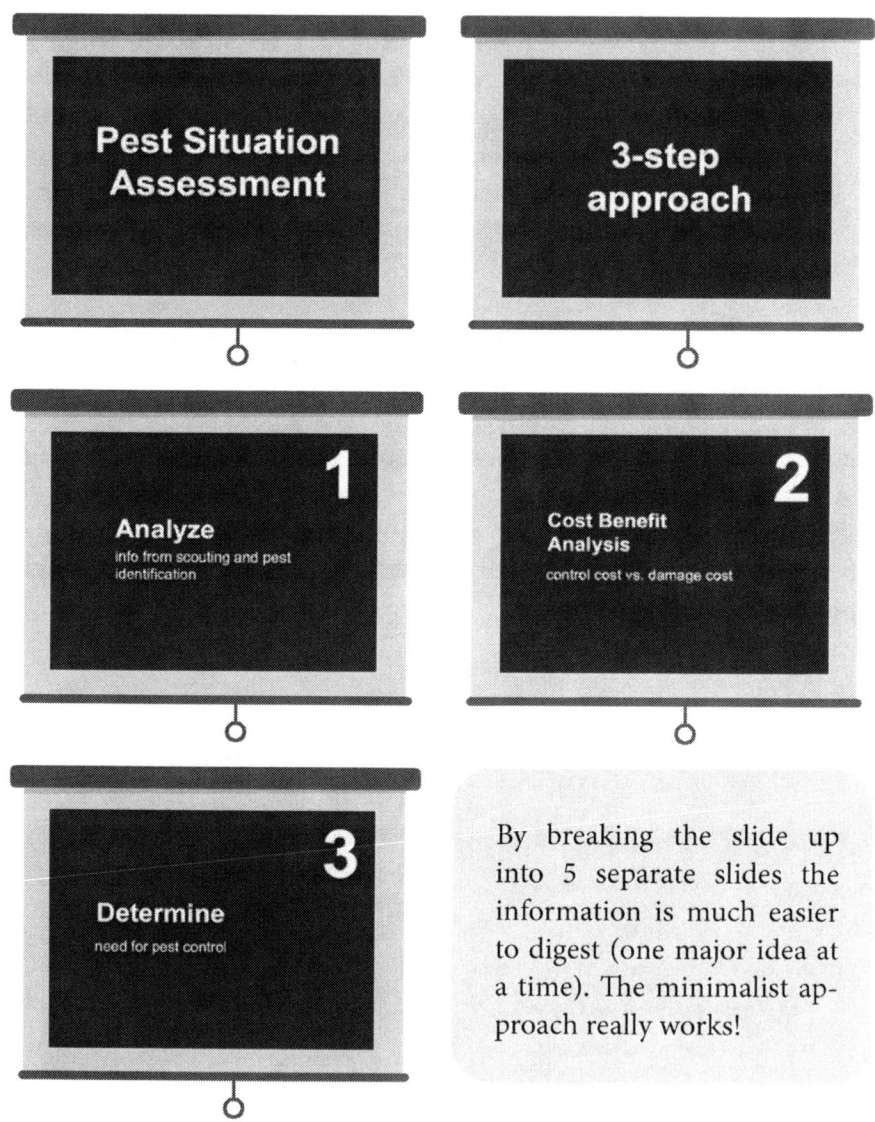

By breaking the slide up into 5 separate slides the information is much easier to digest (one major idea at a time). The minimalist approach really works!

 **EXERCISE:**

Take one of the "ugly" slides that you have found in your "old presenta-tions" deck. Give yourself the 5-minute challenge (with pen and paper).

How could you change the design rapidly here? Do it with pen and paper. (if you cannot find an ugly slide – go to Interlude: straight from the PowerPoint "Horror Files", and take one from one of the "typologies")

_____

_____

_____

_____

_____

_____

_____

_____

Re-use and re-purpose: build your presentation component library

If you want to make visually appealing slides quickly then build up your own library. Then you can re-use slides, charts or approaches rather than reinventing the wheel each time you create a presentation. This may seem like an obvious point, but do you do it?

Creating a library means cataloguing your slides. A library is by defi-nition a body of information that is classified and searchable. You can classify your slides in various ways. You can create separate folders for:

» **All images you've ever used**
» **All charts you've ever used**
» **By type of presentation**

The point is save AND classify. By taking the extra step to classify your slides and components, you'll be able to save even more time (you won't waste time looking for things).

By the way, the presentations don't necessarily have to all be by you. If you find something that could be useful in the future, just save it. As long as you respect copyrights and attribute properly there's no reason why you can't re-use material from other people.

Just be aware of these dangers:

» Especially if you're presenting to the same audience repeatedly, there's a risk that your slides could appear redundant or repetitive. Like a good marriage, occasionally spice up your slides with fresh material or fresh design elements.

» Please avoid the temptation to skip the first steps (the P, O and I of the POINT Program) and go straight to your library before thinking.

Develop a "trademark" design

Every time you present it's a "moment of truth". You have the opportunity to make a good impression that will persuade your audience, enhance your career or bolster your reputation. By developing a "trademark" design you can establish your personal brand. People will recognize and remember the slides, charts, and other visual elements of your presentation. For example, you might be remembered for using funny or shocking full-screen pictures, a particular sans serif font or minimalist slides.

IN "NO-NONSENSE SLIDE DESIGN" YOU LEARNED:

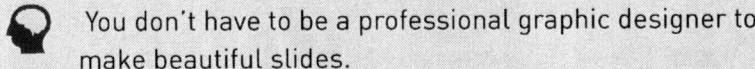

- You don't have to be a professional graphic designer to make beautiful slides.

- Dare to ditch the corporate design – use all of your screen real estate.

- Black is beautiful – sometimes black out your screen to underline your point and connect deeply with the audience.

- Less is more – continually strive to reduce information density.

- A picture paints a thousand words...and can impact your audience on a visceral level.

- Re-use and re-purpose slides and components from your library.

- Develop a "trademark" design to establish and enhance your personal brand.

Case story: no more nonsense for Jo Ann

 "Thank God I can finally open PowerPoint," said Jo Ann with a sly grin. "I was starting to have PowerPoint withdrawal symptoms."

The two women went back to the SmartPresenter's office to get Jo Ann's laptop.

 "Now you can take the messages you've designed and in a very targeted and fast way put them into slides," said Nicole.

"Ok, let me start." Jo Ann whipped up the first slide and the corporate template.

 "Whoa! Whoa! What are you doing there? What is that ugly thing?" said Nicole, her cynical sense of humor re-surfacing.

 "Well, I'm using the company logo and standard design template..."

 "Ditch that!" said Nicole.

"What was your key message again?" asked Nicole.

"Right. And then we add the chart with a nice table after this one, in case people have questions," said Nicole.

"Let's work on this one with the 'radio' budget. Here I believe a good visual will help, and you can then add your key message. Let's quickly go to www.istockphoto.com to find a great picture for this."

"So, what do you think of this slide?" asked Jo Ann.

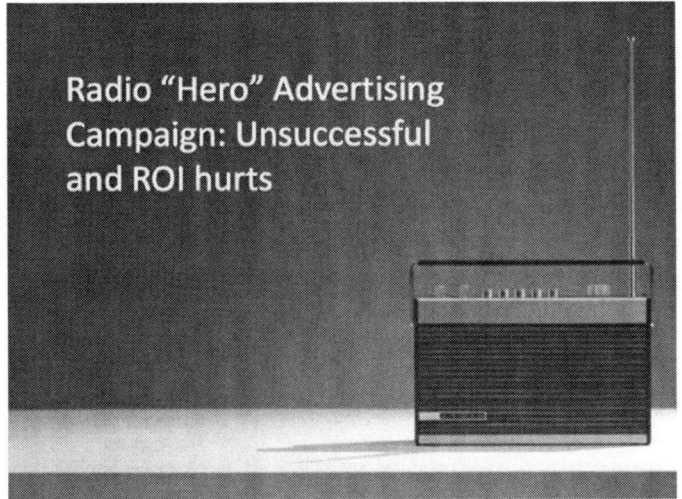

Nicole and Jo Ann worked another 50 minutes on completing the presentation, always using the structured approach, as summarized on the next pages.

Objective	Key Messages	Submessages supporting the key messages	Information Design
"At the end of the presentation, I want to get the 'green light' for next year budget's proposal as well as to have instilled confidence in my team's budgeting and marketing abilities"	"Budgets on track: We have been good and successful budget managers this year"	Budgets are on track and no overspend over limit	First: Statement of key message; In addition, for detailed-oriented people: graph or table that shows what the detailed budget looked like.
	"Majority of activities meets ROI objective; however, not all activities are created equal"	26 marketing initiatives in total; 80% above allowed threshold Some initiatives stand out for good (TV) and bad (radio) results	Show graphic representation of all activities, ideally via bar chart; Show the total and proportion of success; Add specific stories of best and worst performer to go in depth to bring the data to life Show graphic representation of the total channel analysis

No-nonsense slide design proposal	Slide Drawing / example	Slide/design comments from the author
Slide with only key message on it - nothing else; black & white	This Year's Budget was on track	Reduced content, and black background with white text... this also serves as the indicator of past and future. Focus only on key message; Can be created in 1 minute
Slide with detailed backup for "left brainer" (it is a budget presentation after all); change of background color to white to show that there is a change (backup); clearly structure the table so that the eye can follow easily	This Year's Budget was on track	Notice that we have thrown out the standard design and logo; Table was taken from previous presentation, numbers adapted
Visual representation of all activities ranked by their financial result, including the sub message	80%+ of 26 activities ahead of our ROI objective of 3.0	Clear distinction between above and below target; key message on top, below that the chart
Slide with full picture on it, using full real estate and clearly highlighting the 'radio'	Radio "Hero" Advertising Campaign: Unsuccessful and ROI hurts	Visual for story - seeing the radio immediately brings to life which channel was not right... This then needs to be explained with a verbal story
Slide with picture and core message on it, using full real estate and clearly highlighting the 'Mr. Handsome' Campaign	"Mr Handsome": TV campaign appealing to consumers and driving ROI to 5.0	Photo searched and purchased at istockpho-to.com; added to storage for potential re-use in other presentations
Slide with bar chart that summarizes the analysis of all activities; Horizontal bar charts are especially useful for this	Summary ROI per channel	Analytical summary, simple and powerful. Clearly points out the above average channels. Chart newly designed with MS Power-point; The 'Average' bar is singled out to make a visual distinction

Objective	Key Messages	Submessages supporting the key messages	Information Design
"At the end of the presentation, I want to get the 'green light' for next year budget's proposal as well as to have instilled confidence in my team's budgeting and marketing abilities"	"Next year: Flat budget vs. this year, but reshuffled according to this year's insights"	As per guidance, we want to keep the budgets flat; we want to reshuffle between activity pools, based on insights; Less radio & events; More TV and Social Media	Statement of key message Chart data visualization of next year vs. this year, showing proportions and impact Horizontal bar chart; making key changes in budget allocation clear with support, e.g. arrows
	"We want to continue and expand TV and increase Social Media"	Increase Social Media Investments Continue & increase TV investments Introduce Mrs. Handsome	Show Specific and detailed case studies, stories and proposal... Go in-depth to bring it to life; supported by pictures
	Can we have your approval for this budget and plan?		Verbal statement and making the close; handle all discussion points

No-nonsense slide design proposal	Slide Drawing / example	Slide/design comments from the author
Statement on Slide; clear transition vs. before, e.g. via black slide	Next Year we want to fuel sales growth... ...but with flat total budget!	Clear divide - we are in the future now, and that is the key message Chart design same as above first slide, copy & paste and adapted
Horizontal bar chart on full slide, including the sub message; arrows indicate the change in allocation	Proposal for Next Year Total Flat & Focus on highest ROI	Referring back to before channels, information is used to indicate where changes are Chart e.g. copy & pasted from previous presentation, numbers & title adapted
Visual of Mr. Handsome and the change, Mrs. Handsome; Mrs. Handsome picture is introduced with an effect	Continuing "Mr Handsome" And Introducing "Mrs Handsome"	Again full visual only, this allows for background and detailed storytelling by the presenter; Introducing Mrs. Handsome is the only 'entrance effect' in the entire presentation
Visual of Social Media	Increase Investment in Social Media Advertising	Picture was licensed from istockphoto.com Notice the shadow overlay to make the text visible; you can do this by inserting a box and making it transparent
Black slide		This allows full focus on the discussion, It does not distract, it is clear that the presentation has come to an end and that all eyes should be on the presenter now

9 POINT: 'T' is for 'Turning to you'

Unfortunately, most people work on preparing their PowerPoint slides up until the last minute, leaving little or no time for rehearsal. Instead of rehearsing, these people rely on their slides as a teleprompter.

This adds to the litany of boring and incomprehensible presentations, the ones we all have sat through innumerable times.

When you apply the P, O, I and N of the POINT methodology, however, you don't have to be one of these people. You'll free up time to really rehearse. Now you can reinvest some of the time you've saved – in yourself.

This rehearsal and fine-tuning time is extremely important, and extremely powerful. It has great ROI.

We have seen presentations where people stopped tinkering with their slides to rehearse just 30 minutes before delivering their presentation. And these 30 minutes made a dramatic difference. The sentences and messages were spoken smoothly, and the slides and the presenter seemed to be "in sync".

The following are no-nonsense rules on how you should interact with slides and your audience. We will also give some tips on body language.

You and technology

AVOID EMBARRASSMENT

Eight years ago Lars was tinkering with his slides just before a training he had to give in front of 40 managers. He rushed into the presentation hall just in time to take the podium. It was only when he started booting his computer that he noticed that it was about to hibernate. Lars had a very slow computer so he had to reboot it and open all the programs again. The whole exercise took about two minutes, but the two minutes seemed like two hours. To make matters worse, it was Lars' first interaction with the group. Talk about first impressions! Needless to say, the training was a huge failure. But it taught Lars a valuable lesson:

 ALWAYS CHECK YOUR TECHNOLOGY SETUP!

How many of us have failed to take this precaution much to our detriment and embarrassment?

Put simply: when equipment doesn't work you lose valuable time and look unprofessional. Be there early. Check that everything is working. Check the beamer connection, and check if it's working with your computer. Don't leave anything to chance. Check it and check it yourself.

AN ASPIRING "PERFECTIONIST" CRASHES AND BURNS!

At the beginning of Paul's career at Microsoft, his boss asked him to give a presentation to CIOs in Tokyo. He was to present the new features of Windows 3.1 with a special focus on the Japanese version. Seeing this as his "big break", Paul spent hours and hours preparing gorgeous PowerPoint slides complete with screenshots and animations.

The big day arrived and with great nervousness Paul walked into a large roomful of 100 CIOs. And his two bosses were there, too. The organizer of the evening introduced Paul with the slightly sarcastic comment that he had a "real horse and pony show" (referring no doubt to the fancy, overdone slides) in store for them.

Paul completed his presentation without mishap, and started his demo. Unfortunately, his colleague had switched hardware on him at the last moment. Paul was using an NEC 98 ("kyuu hachi") series PC with an unfamiliar keyboard layout and other differences. When Windows didn't respond he started clicking impatiently. The system hanged and there was an awkward silence as Paul tried frantically to recover the situation. In the end he had to re-boot.

What accounted for this spectacular failure? Looking back, it can mainly be attributed to spending too much time making fancy slides rather than thinking about what the audience really wanted to know and see. They mostly wanted an informative presentation and demo, rather than slick slides. Paul should also have checked and re-checked his technology (albeit unhelpful colleagues were a problem).

In any case, you can imagine how demoralized Paul was after that embarrassing episode. But it didn't stop there. One year later he was talking with a CIO who said: "do you remember that bozo who crashed Windows?"

Paul turned red and said nothing.

And check more than just beamers. If there is a sound system, check it as well.

If this sounds time consuming, it is. However, if something is not working during your presentation, you might want to blame the technician. But do you know whom your audience will blame? Exactly: you.

In addition, make sure that nothing is obstructing the beamer and that your slides display promptly and correctly. Lars once followed a training session during which a water glass was placed right before the beamer: one third of the screen was obscured because of this. And as the presenter was an "audience lover" (see below), he did not notice it until somebody from the audience finally had the courage to politely tell him what the issue was.

 EXERCISE

Write down at least 2 examples where there were "technology issues" in the presentations that you gave or have attended. How could these things have been avoided?

You and the screen

PowerPoint is a powerful technology, but in the end it's just a visual aid. You, the speaker, and your message, are what are important. You should be PowerPoint's master not its slave. And one of the most important ways to "tame the PowerPoint beast" is to master your interaction with the screen.

"You should be PowerPoint's master, not its slave."

Over the years, we've observed that there are 3 types of PowerPoint "screen slaves":

» **SCREEN LOVER**

The screen lover faces the screen and reads his slides. He almost hugs the screen, totally or largely ignoring the audience. Think about if you have ever experienced such a presentation. Can you remember how you felt…? Did you feel like the presenter was delivering a monologue? Did you feel disconnected? Exactly. And that's why we recommend that you never do this to your audience. Presenters often fall into the "screen lover" mode when they feel insecure and want to be sure of their words. This combined with monstrous slides is a very bad combination.

» **AUDIENCE LOVER**

The audience lover is the screen lover's opposite. She engages 100% with the audience, rarely if ever looking at or interacting with her slides. It's often not even clear how the slides fit in with her presentation; they're more like background information, yet they never fail to disturb or distract the audience. Very often these presenters could ditch their slides altogether. The only reason they have PowerPoint is…well, because one needs PowerPoint for a presentation, right?

» **TENNIS SPECTATOR**

Have you ever observed fans watching a tennis match? Their heads swivel back and forth. This is the case with the "tennis spectator". He's prone to whipping his head back and forth between the screen and the audience, again and again. It can be very distracting.

TOUCH-TURN-TALK

Fortunately, there's a simple way to both refer to your slides while engaging fully with the audience. It's called "touch-turn-talk". What you do, quite simply, is point to information on your slides then turn back to the audience to make your point(s). Sometimes you may want your audience to focus on your slides since that's where the action is; that's where your point is being made. At other times you may want your audience to focus on you, particularly when you are underlining an important point, telling a story or wish to establish a deeper emotional connection with your audience.

Touch-turn-talk prevents you from falling into the trap of becoming a screen lover, audience lover or tennis spectator. Instead, you'll interact seamlessly with the screen and your audience, and spend 95+% of the time with the people that matter most: the audience.

"PRESENTER VIEW"

In case you are really worried about your notes and the text, and the time, and everything else, then you'll want to take advantage of "Presenter View". Presenter View is a neat feature in PowerPoint that lets you see not only the current slide, but also the time elapsed, the notes you have added to your slides, and the next slide to come. Very handy, indeed!

POINTERS

Some people like to use laser pointers, but we're not big fans of them. The tiny pinpoint of light is often not visible enough, particularly when you're presenting in a large hall to 200 conference delegates. Another disadvantage is that your hand and the little beam of light may shake even when you're not nervous.

Imagine how much they'll shake when you really ARE nervous. It's very noticeable!

We recommend instead that you physically point to or gesture at your slides, if possible. Even in a larger venue, it should be possible to roughly gesture at your slides. In any case, if your slides are well-designed to begin with, it shouldn't be necessary to precisely point out to which piece of information you are currently referring. Of course, if animating your slides makes sense, then do so and you won't need to worry about pointing to particular pieces of information.

ADVANCED SLIDE HANDLING

Advancing slides can often be a hassle. You may have to hunch over a table, run back to your laptop or stay chained to your laptop when you could be roaming around on stage or even mixing with the audience. Sometimes speakers rely on other people to advance their slides but this is very distracting (as in "Next slide, please") and in the worst case the numbskull advancing your slides may advance them too quickly thereby completely messing up your rhythm and sometimes even spoiling a good story or surprise that you had in store for the audience.

There is a better way. We highly recommend purchasing a remote control device. Not a wireless mouse (which is not intended as a presentation device) but a wireless remote control such as those made by Logitech. These handy little devices can slip into your pocket and allow you to do things like advance or go back in your presentation, time your presentation or blackout the screen.

BLACKOUT

As mentioned earlier, sometimes it's more effective simply to blackout the screen. That way you can draw the audience's full attention to you and your message. Depending upon the type of speech and the point in your presentation, this can be a very effective technique, a technique that is made possible by the "blackout" button on your remote control device.

You and you

Rehearsal helps you develop the instincts of a great performer. And these are crucial for really getting your message across. Ultimately, presentation is about you, and not the technology.

Hence now it is time to reinvest. You should reinvest the time you save by applying the POINT program in: practice, practice and practice!

What does the average presenter do? Either most people finish tinkering with their slides 5 minutes before the beginning of the presentation, and then rush directly into the presentation room, or they go through their slides and rehearse them mentally, perhaps mouthing the words silently at best. Mumbling the words under your breath is better but still not good enough.

Speaking to your self simply doesn't do the job. For one thing, you won't get the same feeling in terms of tone, vocal variety, rhythm and projection. Secondly, if you're timing your speech it will take much less time when you go through it mentally than when you speak it out loud. We've learned this the hard way.

So do yourself a favor: stand up and speak the words aloud as if it were for real. Do it as if it's a dress rehearsal. There is simply no better way to prepare for your presentation.

It's worth investing at least 30 minutes in rehearsing. Rehearsing will also let you develop and refine your signature presentation style in terms of your choice of words, timing or rhythm/cadence, and humor.
If you can, try taping yourself on video or audio. Most people feel awkward seeing themselves on video, but don't you want to know how you come across to other people?

Here are a few tips for good delivery:

» **MAKE A GOOD FIRST IMPRESSION**

Dress for success. Take the time in the morning (or better yet, the evening before) to select your clothes for the day. What should you wear? Is it appropriate for the audience? Do you feel comfortable? There are some great style guides out there, and if this is an area of concern for you we suggest that you consult them, or even better, that you find a good style coach or image consultant and get some direct feedback on your own style. It's worth it.

» **EMPTY YOUR POCKETS AND DON'T FIDGET**

Empty all your pockets of loose change and other things that you might fiddle with such as badges, necklaces and pens. Fiddling is unconscious and almost uncontrollable – so just remove the temptation (anyway, your hands should never be in your pockets unless there's a specific reason for them to be there). The audience doesn't want to hear the "bling bling" of coins or "click-clack" of pens.

» **DEAL WITH STAGE FRIGHT**

This is one of the questions we often get. The best way to deal with stage fright is to practice. Just a few minutes invested in a few dry runs will go a long way toward reducing or eliminating stage fright. If you can, also try to engineer a shift in your attitude: be present and try to enjoy the moment. Remember: the best way to overcome a fear is to confront it – which means preparation, practice, and giving lots of presentations. Also, try breathing deeply several times before your presentation and practice relaxation techniques.

» **EYE CONTACT**

Maintain good eye contact but beware the watchtower – avoid continuously scanning the audience as if you're watching a tennis match. At the other extreme, it's ok to give certain people more time, but don't stare like you're a stalker! Always include everybody in the audience. Don't talk to just one person or one side of the room.

» **KEEP YOUR HANDS AT HOME**
Keep them in their natural zone. Learn how to be at ease with your hands at your side and by making appropriate gestures (without overdoing it, depending upon the culture of your audience and the context of your presentation)

» **MOVE WITH PURPOSE**
Find the right balance. Be neither a static "Roman statue" nor a restless "tiger in the cage". Instead, "walk with purpose". That means being very conscious of your movement. Sometimes it's very appropriate and effective to move, even venturing into the audience itself in extreme cases. At other times, it's more appropriate to remain relatively stationary. A great performer knows how to use voice, movement and expression consciously. Nothing is left to chance.

 EXERCISE

Now it's rehearsal time. Take the speech for which you have developed the key messages. Polish it. Create the PowerPoint slides for it. And then get a video camera or digital camera with video function and videotape yourself giving your presentation.

Now watch it with a friend or colleague. What are your strengths as a presenter? What are your "points for improvement". We know it's hard. We know you may wish that you didn't sound so "bad" or look so nervous, or be surprised that you do. But nothing beats watching yourself delivering a presentation. If you cannot find a friend to do this with, go find a professional speech coach or join Toastmasters, the public speaking organization (www.toastmasters.org).

Presentation is a performance and as with a theater play it helps to do a dry run or a dress rehearsal. Your costume, the stage and the lighting are all important factors, but ultimately, it's you – the actor or actress – who will make the performance lively and memorable.

VIDEO NEVER LIES

One of the best ways to practice is to have yourself videotaped. There is nothing more powerful than watching yourself on video.

Lars' experience is a case in point. As a young 20 year old, he was preparing for a 10-minute presentation he had to give as part of his internship. He gave the presentation (which was recorded on video) and thought he'd done pretty well. In hindsight, Lars admits that perhaps he was a bit over-confident.

The trainers told him that he had been mumbling and that they couldn't understand him. "Hogwash!" thought Lars to himself.

When he saw himself on video, however, the truth became apparent. "Oh!" he thought as he noticed how he barely looked at the audience, fidgeted with his hands and mumbled.

Facing the truth of his suboptimal performance, Lars focused on improving, and his performance the next day was much better. He even received compliments from the audience.

No one likes watching themselves on video. It's awkward or even painful. But there's no better way to see where you need to improve.

For tips on giving feedback, please refer to the checklist in the appendix.

IN "TURNING TO YOU" YOU LEARNED

 Always check your technology beforehand.

 Use "touch-turn-talk" to interact with your slides

 Invest in a remote control device to advance slides or blackout the screen.

 When appropriate, blackout the screen to focus attention on you and your message.

 Invest in rehearsal and remember that ultimately, only you – the speaker – can deliver a stunning performance.

Case story: Jo Ann realizes that practice DOES make perfect!

Jo Ann finished her presentation, with help from Nicole, and now she didn't know what to do with herself. She didn't have anything to read and had already checked her email. She'd never finished preparing a presentation in so little time.

Just then the SmartPresenter walked in.

 "How was your session?" he asked.

 "Great! Nicole really helped me a lot…My presentation is already done and it looks much better than the one I took six hours to make. Well, I won't take anymore of your time. Thank you." Jo Ann stood up, preparing to leave.

 "Whoa! Not so fast," said the SmartPresenter. "There's still work to be done. Now it's time to re-invest some of the time you saved on preparing your presentation."

 "What do you mean?" Jo Ann interrupted. "I'm done. The presentation is ready."

 "Well…have you practiced it?"

 "What for? It's ready…I usually just read through my presentations a few times," said Jo Ann, wondering what was coming next.

 "Let me explain something to you," said the SmartPresenter. "The 4 steps we've gone through to prepare your presentation are really important and in my view the cornerstone of a great presentation. However, real impact only comes from great content together with great delivery. That's why you should take some of the time you

saved and re-invest it in practicing. It's true what they say: practice does make perfect."

 *"But I already read through my slides..." protested Jo Ann.*

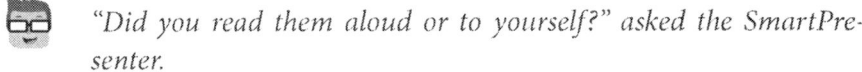 *"Did you read them aloud or to yourself?" asked the SmartPresenter.*

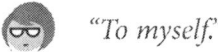 *"To myself."*

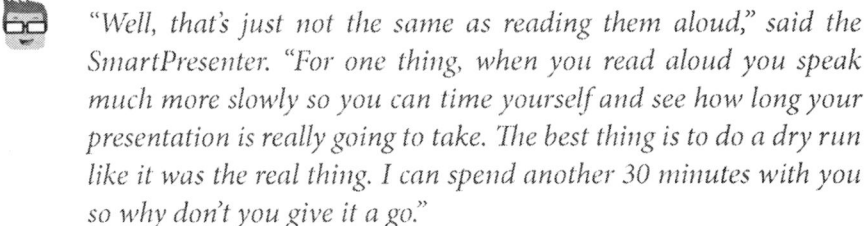 *"Well, that's just not the same as reading them aloud," said the SmartPresenter. "For one thing, when you read aloud you speak much more slowly so you can time yourself and see how long your presentation is really going to take. The best thing is to do a dry run like it was the real thing. I can spend another 30 minutes with you so why don't you give it a go."*

Jo Ann gave her presentation.

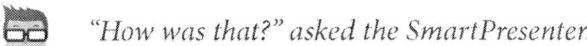 *"How was that?" asked the SmartPresenter.*

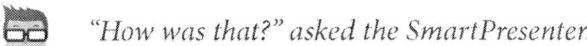 *"Ok, but I stumbled over my words and didn't feel totally comfortable."*

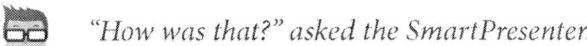 *"Ok, do it again then."*

Jo Ann gave her presentation again.

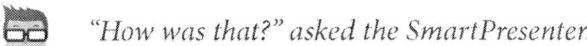 *"How did it feel now?" asked the SmartPresenter.*

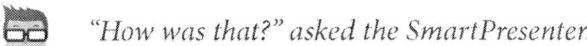 *"Much better," said Jo Ann. "It was much smoother."*

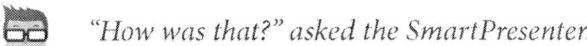 *"Aha! And how long did that take now?" asked the SmartPresenter.*

"Only about 30 minutes..." said Jo Ann with a hint of surprise in her voice.

 "Yet these 30 minutes are key..." chimed in the SmartPresenter.

Jo Ann thanked the SmartPresenter for his time and offered to buy him lunch sometime. She drove back to her office. It had been quite an interesting day. She'd learned a lot from some rather colorful characters, Nicole and the SmartPresenter.

That Friday, Jo Ann got a second chance to deliver her budget presentation.

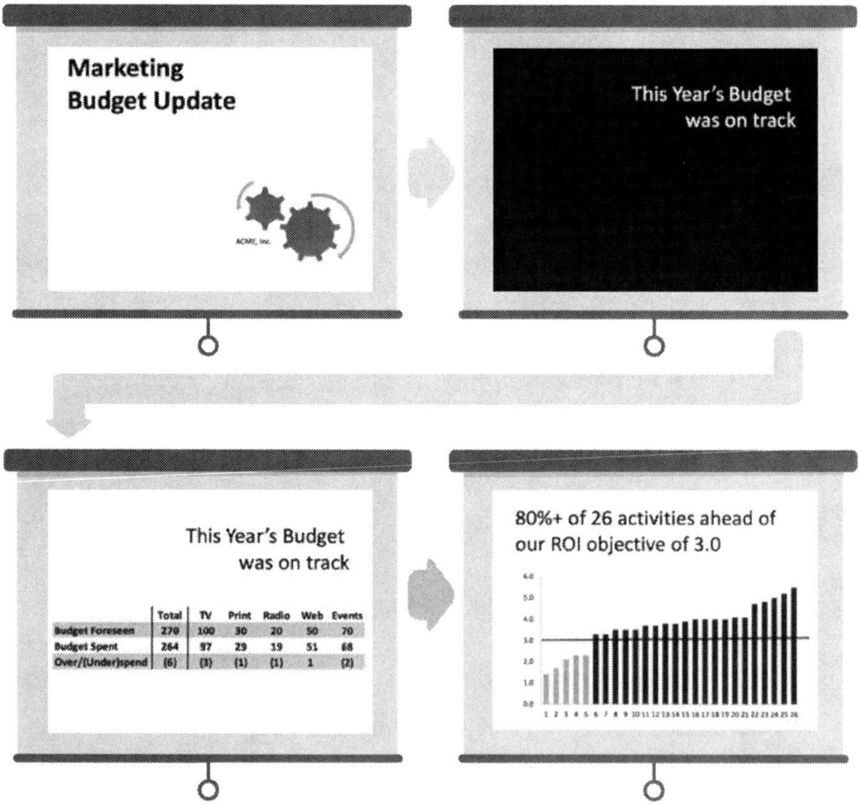

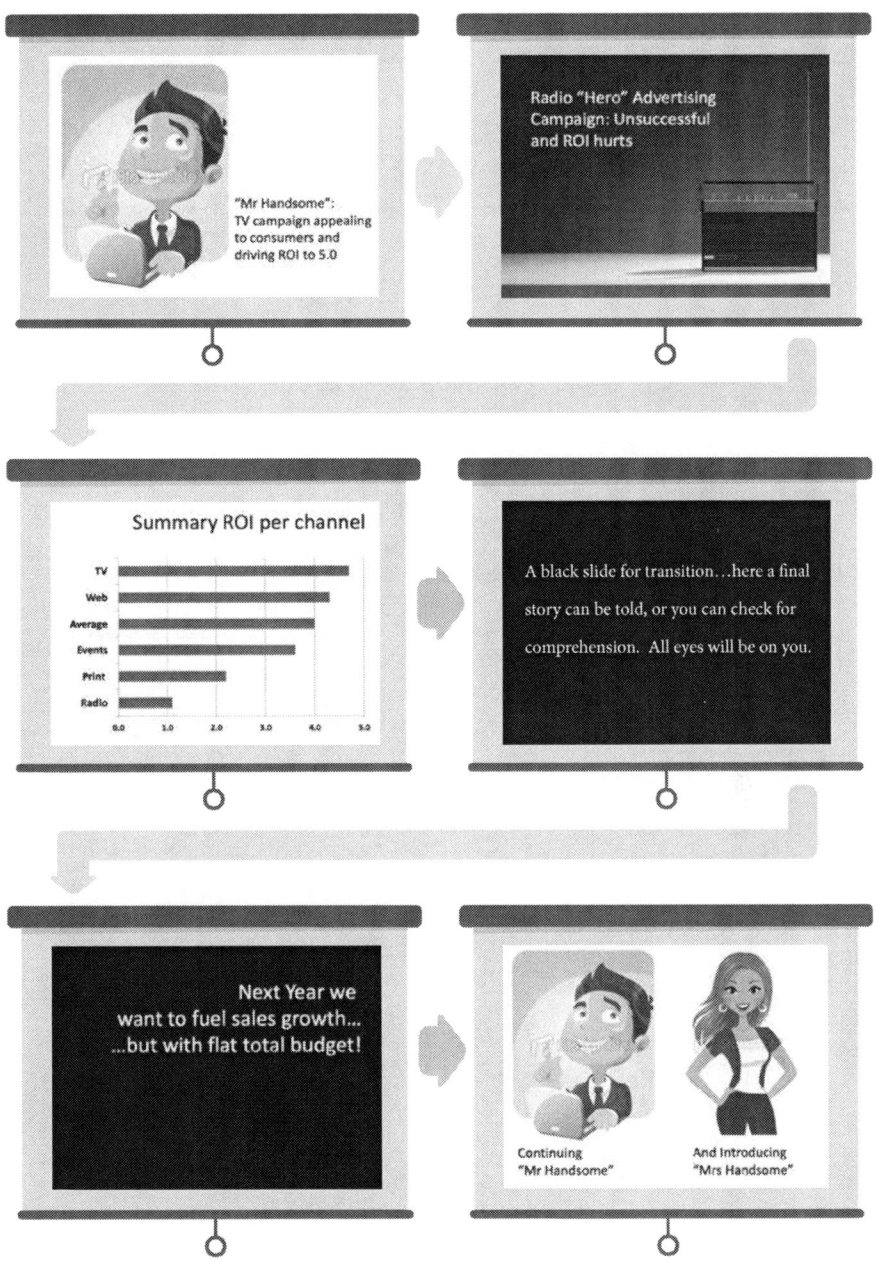

It went so well that people even clapped at the end.

She'd definitely have to take the SmartPresenter to a really nice restaurant to thank him.

For a full analysis of Jo Ann's speech and her presentation before & after, see the appendix.

10 The Smart Presenter as performer

"Marcus Tullius Cicero - the great Roman orator, philosopher, statesman, lawyer, political theorist and consul - once said:"

Cicero
(citing Antonius in On the Orator, Vol. I, Ch. 27)

"In an orator ... we demand the acuteness of a logician, the profundity of a philosopher, the diction virtually of a poet, the memory of a lawyer, the voice of a performer in tragic drama, the gestures, you might almost say, of an actor at the very top of his profession. Here, then, are some of the reasons why a first-class orator is one of the rarest things in the world."

We don't expect you to become a "first-class orator" overnight, but by following all of the tips from The SmartPresenter you should improve and save time dramatically. We're convinced that you'll be able to double your impact and halve your preparation time. Several of our clients have used this methodology to transform their performance.

But how can you get an extra edge? If there's one thing we hope you've learned from The SmartPresenter it's how to take advantage of what we call "the PowerPoint Paradox". Most people slave over their slides up until the last minute and don't rehearse at all. Then they rely on their slides as a teleprompter.

You don't have to be "most people", however. Paradoxically, by spending less time on the minutiae of your slides and more time at the front end (on thinking about your objectives, messages and organization) and back-end (rehearsing), you can dramatically increase the impact of every presentation you give.

Investing in thinking and practicing will make you a much better presenter than spending time tinkering with slides, don't you think?

Now it's time to reinvest some of the time you save in yourself to really hone your presentation skills.

Here's the virtuous cycle that we have followed in our evolution as speakers:

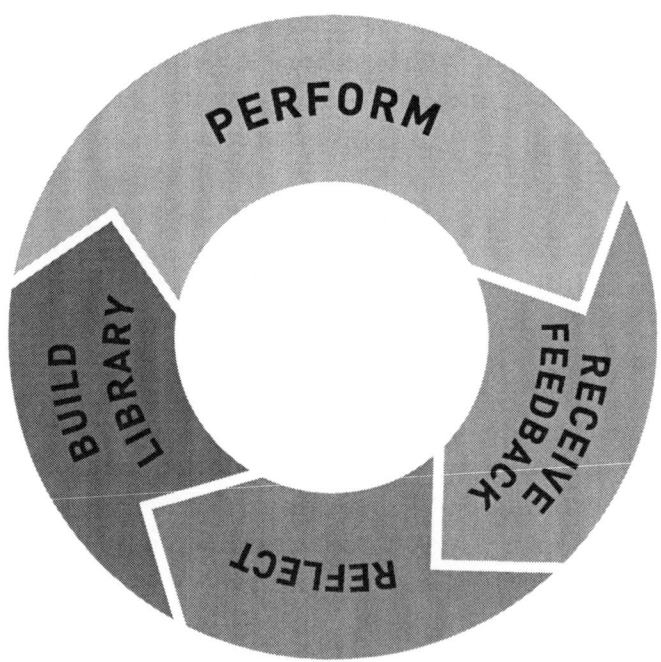

Happy presenting!

11 Appendices

APPENDIX 1: The POINT One Page Summary

(P) POWERFUL OBJECTIVE
Begin with the end in mind. Write down a one-sentence objective. Take the TV interview test. What would you like people to say about your presentation after they've heard it?

(O) ORGANIZE
Remember: when it comes to organization it's NOT "one size fits all". Choose the organization that best conveys your messages. Try the story flow method or refer to the Smart Structure Quick Reference Guide for examples.

(I) INFORMATION DESIGN
Reduce information density and highlight key concepts. Try alternatives to bullet points such as a step-wise approach, a schematic or conceptual diagram, a real or stylized example, a quotation/testimonial, a powerful visual, a movie, props or telling a story.

(N) NO-NONSENSE SLIDE DESIGN
Don't waste valuable screen "real estate". Follow the 10 "no-nonsense slide design" principles

(T) TURNING TO YOU
Check your technology. Touch-turn-talk. Black out the screen to draw attention to you – the speaker – at key moments during your presentation. Time your presentation. Do a dress rehearsal. Practice, practice, practice!

APPENDIX 2: Smart Structure Quick Reference Guide

INTERNAL

» **Project status**

    » **3 Part:** straight 3 parts, e.g. 1) re-statement/review of objectives; 2) analysis of performance against; 3) open issues/steps to be taken.

    » **Chronological:** past, present, projected performance against plan.

» **Financial/performance reporting**

    » **3 Part:** straight 3 parts, e.g. 1) re-statement/review of objectives; 2) analysis of performance against; 3) open issues/steps to be taken.

» **Product briefing**

    » **How to (step-wise):** how it works in a few steps.

    » **Objective-Proof/Reasoning:** we want you to sell more of this product, here's why this product is superior so we think you can sell more.

    » **Problem-Solution:** until now we've had a problem/lack of key functionality/hole in our product line. Now we have the solution with product X.

» **Promise-Problem-Solution:**
imagine [optimistic scenario] but
the reality is [problem]. Here's the
solution.

» **Comparative:** compare (positioning vs.) with other products (either
within a product line or vs. competing products) to highlight the differences or advantages.

» **Topical:** main plus subtopics; e.g.
features, user interface, price.

» **Case/Example/Illustration:** walk
the audience through a scenario of
use.

» Product launch/
marketing campaign

» **How to (step-wise):** how we'll roll
this out, in a few steps.

» **Objective-Proof/Reasoning:** we
want you to drive home this message; here's how.

» **Problem-Solution:** we have an
image problem. That's why we're
launching this campaign.

» **Promise-Problem-Solution:** we want to be perceived as the innovator in x. The problem is that right now consumers see us as stodgy copycats. This is how we're going to overcome that image.

. . . .

» **Comparative:** compare and contrast with other campaigns.

. . . .

» **Case/Example/Illustration:** walk the audience through a sales role play.

. . . .

» Strategy briefing

» **Before & After:** world before, major event or trend, world after => therefore change in strategy; <or> world before, major event or trend plus change in strategy, (projected) world after.

. . . .

» **Cause & Effect:** impact of new strategy, description of strategy and justification for it (e.g. changes in the marketplace).

. . . .

» Investment proposal

» **Objective-Proof/Reasoning:** invest in project X, here's why.

» **Before & After:** before and after change in market position as a result of the investment.

» **Cause & Effect:** start with the result (paint picture of benefits of the investment) then explain how much/what is needed.

» **Promise-Problem-Solution:** "imagine" this result, but here's the problem, and here's the solution (invest and sign here!).

» **Comparative:** could invest in A, B, or C. Here's why A is the best alternative. Often use the other alternatives as "straw men" to make your favored alternative look more desireable.

» Announcing new organizational structure

» **Before & After:** org structure before, why we needed to change it, new structure, implications.

» **Problem-Solution:** problem(s) we faced (sub-optimal performance of the organization), solution (the new organization).

» New legislation briefing	» **3 Part:** straight 3 parts (try to limit to max 5 points, else use an ACRONYM).
	» **Topical:** main plus subtopics; e.g. law plus the areas it impacts such as areas of the business or the sub-clauses of the law.
	» **Cause & Effect:** expected effect or impact, then explain the cause (the new legislation).
» New compliance requirements	» **How to (step-wise):** how to comply in 3-5 steps.
» New manufacturing process	» **How to (step-wise):** how it works in a few steps (break it down into major and minor steps if it's too complex).
	» **Spatial/Chronological:** a journey through space (e.g. assembly line) and/or time (process).
	» **Case/Example/Illustration:** describe production of a real or imaginary product using the process (e.g. one widget).

EXTERNAL

» **Latest financial performance**

    » **Before & After:** performance in the previous financial period, performance in this period.

    » **Comparative:** comparison of financial performance/indicators against industry benchmark or selected competitors.

    » **Topical:** financial performance as measured by key performance indicators.

    » **Question-Answer:** what were the key drivers of our performance in the last financial period? They were...

» **Addressing a controversial issue**

    » **Controversial:** we take full responsibility for x, but not for y. Some say that xxx. We don't agree with x, but we do agree with y. We think that our approach is better because. xxx. So, let's agree on x. And this is what we should all be doing.

» **New product launch**

» **Before & After:** in the old days, you had to do x. With our product, that's a thing of the past.

. . . .

» **Problem-Solution:** until now it's been hard to do x. Now we have the solution with product y.

. . . .

» **Promise-Problem-Solution:** imagine [optimistic scenario] but the reality is [problem]. Here's the solution.

. . . .

» **Merger/Acquisition press briefing**

» **Lists:** e.g. top 5 reasons why we're convinced this merger makes sense.

. . . .

» **Before & After:** before the merger, after the merger (benefits).

. . . .

» **Cause & Effect:** we decided on this merger; this is why.

. . . .

» **Promise-Problem-Solution:** we wanted to enter the market in fast-growing emerging countries, but we had no experience or capabilities in these regions, that's why we're merging with company x.

. . . .

» **Question-Answer:** here are answers to some common questions regarding the merger.

. . . .

» Sales presentation

» **How to:** I'm going to show you how you can use product x to double your sales.

» **Lists:** here are 3 reasons why we think that product x is a good fit for your organization.

» **Problem-Solution:** do you have a problem with? Here's the solution.

» **Promise-Problem-Solution:** imagine being able to x. But you're probably experiencing problems with y. Here's the solution.

» **Objective-Proof:** we think you need product x. Here's why.

» **Cause & Effect:** company x doubled their sales. This is how they did it using product z.

» **Case / Example / Illustration:** here's a story about how this little company doubled their sales by using our proven methodology.

» VC pitch (for funding)

» **Objective-Proof/Reasoning:** invest in project X, here's why.

. . . .

» **Before & After:** before and after change in market position as a result of the investment; before and after return on your investment.

. . . .

» **Cause & Effect:** start with the result (paint picture of what can be realized; e.g. with your investment, we can ramp up manufacturing and enter these new markets) then explain how much/what is needed.

. . . .

» **Promise-Problem-Solution:** "imagine" this result, but here's the problem, and here's the solution (invest and sign here!).

. . . .

» **Comparative:** could invest in A, B, or C. Here's why A is the best alternative. Often use the other alternatives as "straw men" to make your favored alternative look more desirable.

. . . .

» Future vision (company, technology, industry)

» **Problem-Solution:** Houston, we've got a problem! But we can solve it with this technology.

. . . .

» **Promise-Problem-Solution:** imagine being able to do x. But you're probably experiencing problems with y. Here's the solution.

. . . .

» **Before & After:** right now we can only do x; but once we develop this new technology / structure / model we'll be able to do y.

. . . .

» **Case / Example / Illustration:** here's a hypothetical story about the technology of the future – what our world will look like.

. . . .

» **Story:** Dr. Z had a vision, so he did this and realized these results. Now, he's working on x and thinks it will be possible in the future to realize y.

. . . .

APPENDIX 3: The Case Study: Jo Ann becomes a SmartPresenter

» 'P' FOR POWERFUL OBJECTIVE

Remember what we learned about setting a powerful objective? Basically, it can be summed up with the phrase: "begin with the end in mind". Before diving into PowerPoint then, Jo Ann should have instead asked herself a few simple questions.

In this case, she should start by setting a one-sentence objective. Her one sentence objective could be:

"At the end of the presentation, I want to get the 'green light' for next year's budget proposal as well as instill confidence in my team's budgeting and marketing abilities."

That's it. Now if Jo Ann applies the "TV interview test", she can quickly back out her 5 key messages:

"We are good budget managers – this year's budget is on track."

"ROI's by Advertising channel are very different: TV and Web are the best; radio and print are the worst."

"For next year, we want to maintain a flat budget vs. this year (i.e. no growth) and we want to reorder our priorities."

"Going forward, priority should be on continuing and refining the 'handsome' TV ad campaign."

"We want to invest in social media marketing, for example, by introducing a Facebook group."

That's it…these are the key messages that we want to get across, and we have not even touched PowerPoint yet.

» 'O' FOR ORGANIZATION

Let's look at what Jo Ann should do in terms of organization. The original presentation had a flow like this.

> » Old budget status
> » Old budget result
> » Old budget result
> » New budget.

If we analyze this, it becomes obvious that while the overall structure is fine (past and future), the presentation focuses too much on the past instead of on the result we want to achieve.

But the time structure is a very powerful. We can easily map our key messages to this structure:

THE PAST
» Key Message: "Good budget managers"
» Key Message: "Majority of activities meet objective, some are interesting to point out for learning purposes (TV: good; Radio: bad)"
» Key Message: Not all activities are created equally

THE FUTURE
» Key Message: Propose flat budget vs. last year, but reordered priorities based on what we've learned
» Key Message: We want to continue and expand the Mr. Handsome campaign and increase our web presence

This is a good flow, more balanced and in line with our objective. Always check whether your structure helps you to accomplish your objective.

» 'I' FOR INFORMATION DESIGN

Here's an example of the Information Design Template filled in for Jo Ann's presentation. She's clearly identified her key messages, the sub-messages that support them and the information design (how she will structure the messages to express them).

Objective	Key Messages	Submessages supporting	Generic Message Design	Suggested Method
		These depend on time & ROI available - current example desinged for 10 minute		
	"Good budget managers"	Make this big - for all	Verbal Statement; Large Statement	Statement on Slide
		Highlight the facts...for left brainers and right brainers	Graph or Table that shows how much we were on budget, on target	Show a table as backup; only few ; clearly structure the table so that the eye can follow
	"Majority of activities meet objective, some are interesting to point out for learning (TV: good; Radio: bad)"	Show overview of activities in budget context	Show Graphic Representation of all activities; Show the total and proportion of succes	Horizontal bar chart; visually separating the "good from the ugly"
		Give examples, make it real	Stories...go indepth to bring it alive	Two indepth stories, supported by visuals
	"Not all activities are created equally"	Powerful conclusion making suggestions	Analytical...powerful graph that supports the key messages	Bar chart that clearly shows the difference between Activity type
	"Flat budget vs last year, but reshuffled according to learnings"	Make this the big statement	Verbal Statement	Statement on Slide; clear transition vs before
		Show the proposal based on analysis	Chart data vizualisation; showing proportions and impact, potentially with animation	Horizontal bar chart; making key changes highly clear with support
	"We want to continue and expand Mr Handsome and increase Web presence"	Give examples...	Stories...go indepth to bring it alive	Two indepth stories on the key activities that will change, supported by visuals and animation - make it alive

» 'N' FOR NO-NONSENSE SLIDE DESIGN

After thinking through the first three parts of the POINT methodology, only now do we actually need to touch PowerPoint. Notice how late this comes in the process. The beauty of working this way is that once you've done all the preliminary work, actually creating the slides can go very fast. Mozart composed entire symphonies in his head before putting pen to paper.

Jo Ann knows what she wants, so she goes to her database to see what's already there. She uses her trademark design and approach. Where a message is new, she knows how to quickly create it. There's a lot less tinkering involved.

So, what could Jo Ann do with our messages above? You can see how we have integrated all the messages in the flow below.

Key Messages	Suggested Method for this case	Slide proposal	Comments
"Good budget managers"	Statement on slide	This Year's Budget was on track	Reduced content, and black background with white text... this also serves as the indicator of past and future. Focus only on key message.
	Show a table as backup; only few; clearly structure the table so that the eye can follow	This Year's Budget was on track	Backup slide for the "left brain" people (it is a budget presentation after all) Chose a table here to demonstrate the indepth understanding of budgets. Notice that we have thrown out the standard design and logo - you have already shown this on the first slide; also... the passion statement is out. Table was taken from previous presentation, numbers adapted
"Majority of activities meet objective, some are interesting to point out for learning (TV: good; Radio: bad)"	Horizontal bar chart; visually separating the "good from the ugly"	80%+ of 26 activities ahead of our ROI objective of 3.0	Visual representation of all activities ranked by their financial result; clear distinction between above and below target... Key message on top, after that chart
	2 indepth stories, supported by visuals	Radio "Hero" Advertising Campaign: Unsuccessful and ROI hurts	Visual for story... Seeing the radio immediately brings to life which channel was not right... This then needs to be filled by a verbal story; Foto for radio searched and purchased at istockphoto.com
"Not all activities are created equally"	Bar chart that clearly shows the difference between activity type	Summary ROI per channel	Analytical summary, simple and powerful. Clearly points out the above average channels. Chart newly designed with MS Powerpoint

Key Messages	Suggested Method for this case	Slide proposal	Comments
"Flat budget vs. last year, but reshuffled according to learnings"	Statement on slide; clear transition vs before	**Next Year we want to fuel sales growth... ...but with flat total budget!**	Clear divide - we are in the future now, and that is the key message Chart design same as above first slide, copy & paste and adapted
	Horizontal bar chart; making key changes highly clear with support	Proposal for Next Year Total Flat & Focus on highest ROI	Referring back to before channels, information is used to indicate where changes are Chart copy & pasted from previous presentation, numbers & title of course adapted
"We want to continue and expand Mr. Handsome and increase Web presence"	Two indepth stories on the key activities that will change, supported by visuals and animation - make it alive	Increase Investment in Social Media Advertising	Picture from private database, was licensed from istockphoto.com for a previous presentation Notice the shadow overlay to make the text visible Not the full use of the real estate - this brings the power to the picture

» 'T' FOR TURNING TO YOU

Since Jo Ann now has spent a lot less time tinkering with her slides she has time to spare to rehearse her presentation. She practices to see how it flows and to make sure the transitions are smooth. Ideally, you should practice at least two days before your actual presentation and do at least two dry runs. Practice doesn't mean reading or mouthing the slides it means really giving the presentation as if it were for real. This is an absolutely vital step. Only if you really do it, and ideally, videotape yourself, will you be able to identify gaps in the flow.

Investing in practice raises both your impact and your presentation ROI, and certainly much more than any last minute tinkering with slides.

JO ANN'S PRESENTATION AFTER APPLYING POINT

Here is Jo Ann's final presentation. We have added the title slide as well as the other examples and nice black transition slides. The "Before" POINT is presented in the left hand column and the "After" POINT in the right hand column.

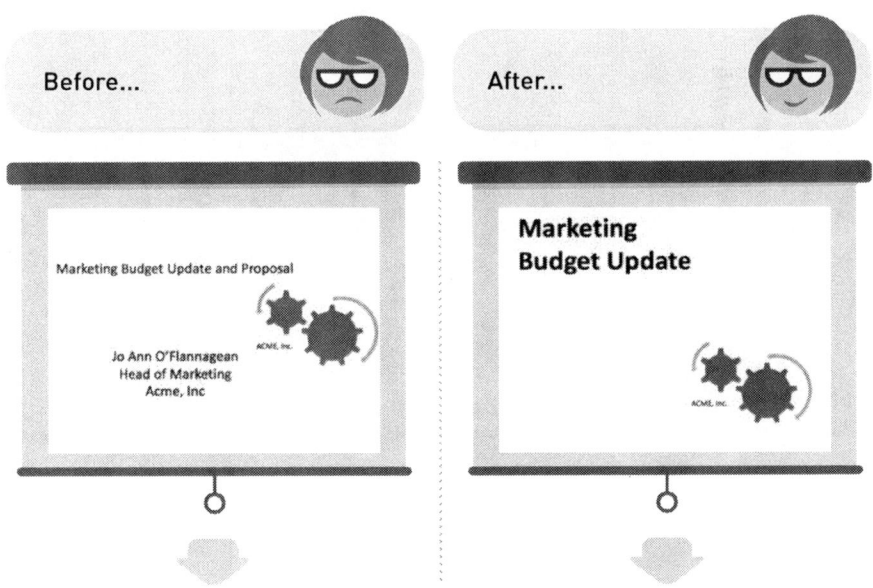

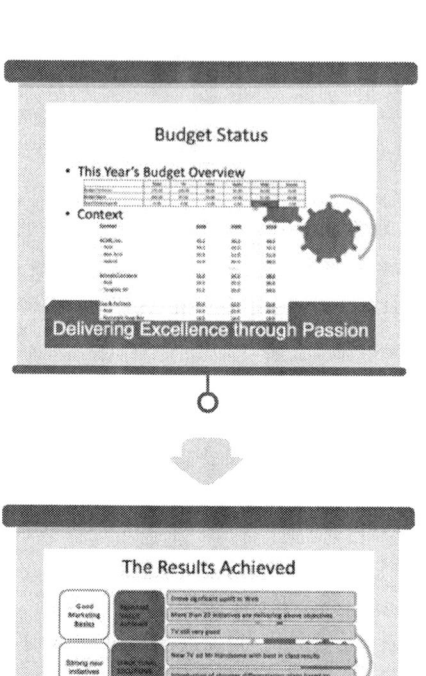

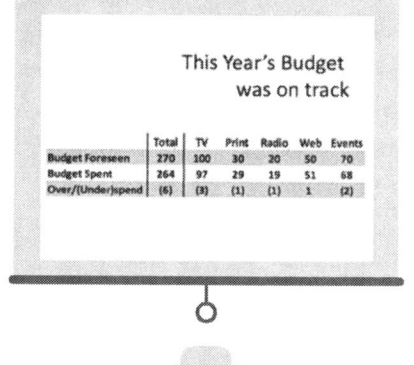

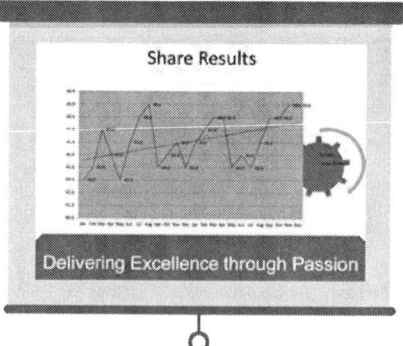

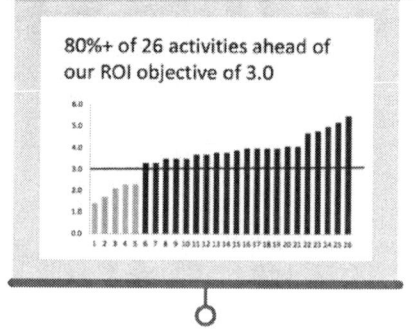

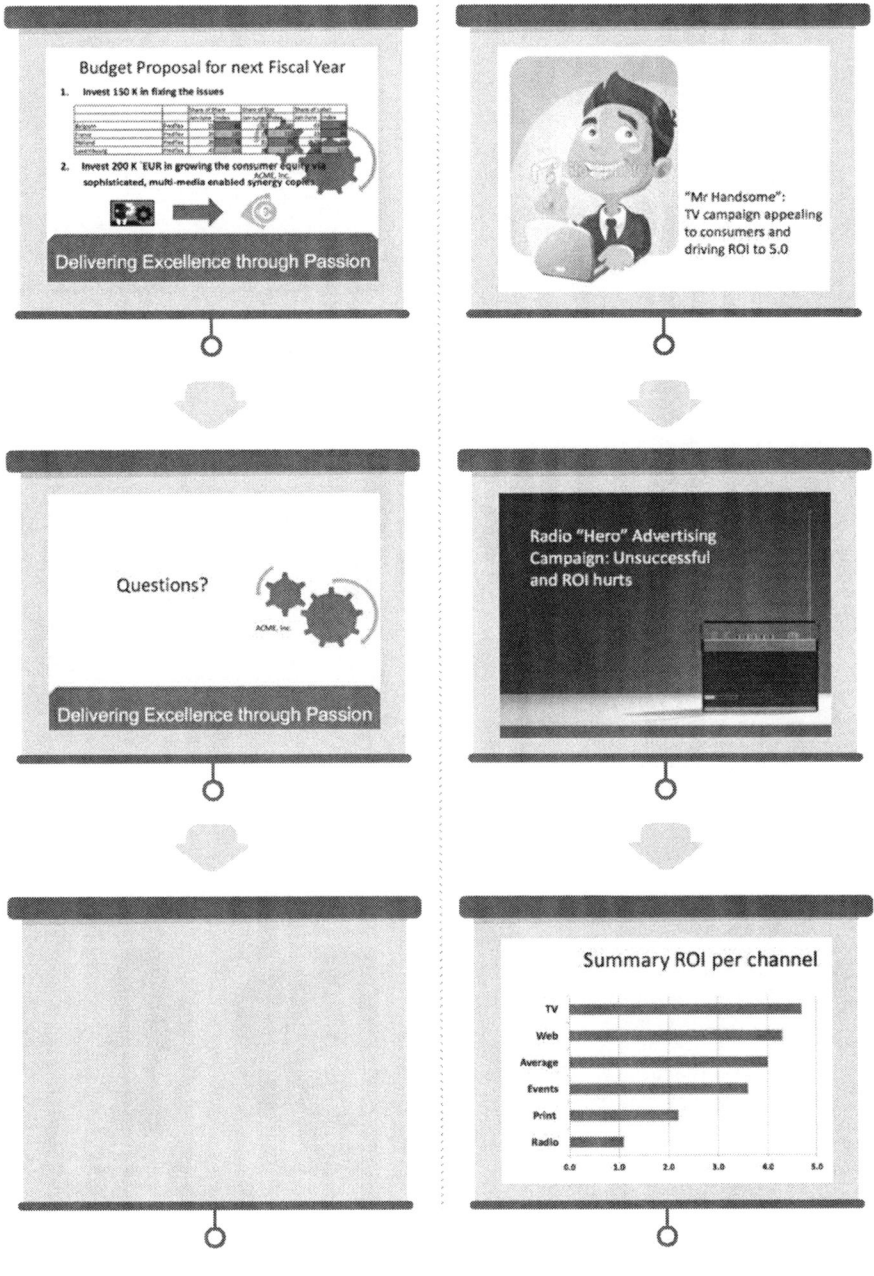

APPENDIX 4: The Information Design Checklist

» Have you reduced the information density of your slides? Can you reduce it further?

» Are the key concepts or messages highlighted?

» Have you used formatting (bold, font size, etc.) to highlight the key concepts?

» Are you using your slides as a visual aid as handouts or as a teleprompter?

» While there is nothing wrong with using bullets per se, have you considered alternative approaches such as a step-wise approach, schematic, example, quotation, powerful visual or story?

» Have you considered using physical props or other visual aids?

APPENDIX 5: Checklist for Giving Feedback

POWERFUL OBJECTIVE
» Was the objective of the presentation clear?
» What were the 3-5 most important messages?

ORGANIZATION
» How was the presentation organized?
» Did you feel guided by the presenter at all times?

INFORMATION DESIGN
» Was the data presented in a compelling way?
» If not, what could be done differently?

NO-NONSENSE DESIGN
» Did you like the slide design?
» Did it enhance and support the key messages?

TURNING TO YOU
» Was the presenter's body language effective?
» How did the presenter use his or her slides?

APPENDIX 6: Template for slide design

Objective	Key Messages	Submessages supporting the key messages	Information Design	No-nonsense Slide Design Proposal	Slide Drawing / Example	Comments

APPENDIX 7: the full, filled-in template for Jo Ann's presentation

Objective	Key Messages	Submessages supporting the key messages	Information Design
"At the end of the presentation, I want to get the 'green light' for next year budget's proposal as well as to have instilled confidence in my team's budgeting and marketing abilities"	"Budgets on track: We have been good and successful budget managers this year"	Budgets are on track and no overspend over limit	First: Statement of key message; In addition, for detailed-oriented people: graph or table that shows what the detailed budget looked like.
	"Majority of activities meets ROI objective; however, not all activities are created equal"	26 marketing initiatives in total; 80% above allowed threshold Some initiatives stand out for good (TV) and bad (radio) results	Show graphic representation of all activities, ideally via bar chart; Show the total and proportion of success; Add specific stories of best and worst performer to go in depth to bring the data to life Show graphic representation of the total channel analysis

No-nonsense slide design proposal	Slide Drawing / example	Slide/design comments from the author
Slide with only key message on it - nothing else; black & white	This Year's Budget was on track	Reduced content, and black background with white text... this also serves as the indicator of past and future. Focus only on key message; Can be created in 1 minute
Slide with detailed backup for "left brainer" (it is a budget presentation after all); change of background color to white to show that there is a change (backup); clearly structure the table so that the eye can follow easily	This Year's Budget was on track	Notice that we have thrown out the standard design and logo; Table was taken from previous presentation, numbers adapted
Visual representation of all activities ranked by their financial result, including the sub message	80%+ of 26 activities ahead of our ROI objective of 3.0	Clear distinction between above and below target; key message on top, below that the chart
Slide with full picture on it, using full real estate and clearly highlighting the 'radio'	Radio "Hero" Advertising Campaign: Unsuccessful and ROI hurts	Visual for story - seeing the radio immediately brings to life which channel was not right... This then needs to be explained with a verbal story
Slide with picture and core message on it, using full real estate and clearly highlighting the 'Mr. Handsome' Campaign	"Mr Handsome": TV campaign appealing to consumers and driving ROI to 5.0	Photo searched and purchased at istockpho-to.com; added to storage for potential re-use in other presentations
Slide with bar chart that summarizes the analysis of all activities; Horizontal bar charts are especially useful for this	Summary ROI per channel	Analytical summary, simple and powerful. Clearly points out the above average channels. Chart newly designed with MS Power-point; The 'Average' bar is singled out to make a visual distinction

Objective	Key Messages	Submessages supporting the key messages	Information Design
"At the end of the presentation, I want to get the 'green light' for next year budget's proposal as well as to have instilled confidence in my team's budgeting and marketing abilities"	"Next year: Flat budget vs. this year, but reshuffled according to this year's insights"	As per guidance, we want to keep the budgets flat; we want to reshuffle between activity pools, based on insights; Less radio & events; More TV and Social Media	Statement of key message Chart data visualization of next year vs. this year, showing proportions and impact Horizontal bar chart; making key changes in budget allocation clear with support, e.g. arrows
	"We want to continue and expand TV and increase Social Media"	Increase Social Media Investments Continue & increase TV investments Introduce Mrs. Handsome	Show Specific and detailed case studies, stories and proposal... Go in-depth to bring it to life; supported by pictures
	Can we have your approval for this budget and plan?		Verbal statement and making the close; handle all discussion points

No-nonsense slide design proposal	Slide Drawing / example	Slide/design comments from the author
Statement on Slide; clear transition vs. before, e.g. via black slide	Next Year we want to fuel sales growth... ...but with flat total budget!	Clear divide - we are in the future now, and that is the key message Chart design same as above first slide, copy & paste and adapted
Horizontal bar chart on full slide, including the sub message; arrows indicate the change in allocation	Proposal for Next Year Total Flat & Focus on highest ROI	Referring back to before channels, information is used to indicate where changes are Chart e.g. copy & pasted from previous presentation, numbers & title adapted
Visual of Mr. Handsome and the change, Mrs. Handsome; Mrs. Handsome picture is introduced with an effect	Continuing "Mr Handsome" And Introducing "Mrs Handsome"	Again full visual only, this allows for background and detailed storytelling by the presenter; Introducing Mrs. Handsome is the only 'entrance effect' in the entire presentation
Visual of Social Media	Increase Investment in Social Media Advertising	Picture was licensed from istockphoto.com Notice the shadow overlay to make the text visible; you can do this by inserting a box and making it transparent
Black slide		This allows full focus on the discussion, It does not distract, it is clear that the presentation has come to an end and that all eyes should be on the presenter now

APPENDIX 8: Further reading

If you want to further explore different areas of business presentations, here are some great books that we recommend:

» **Information Design:**

- Few, Stephen, Show Me the Numbers. Designing Tables and Graphs to Enlighten.
- Zelazny, Gene, Say it with Charts. The Executive's Guide to Visual Communication.
- Tufte, Edward, The Visual Display of Quantitative Information.

» **Slide Design:**

- Duarte, Nancy, slide:ology: The Art and Science of Creating Great Presentations.
- Lidwell, William et al., Universal Principles of Design.
- Reynolds, Garr, Presentation Zen. Simple Ideas on Presentation Design and Delivery.

» **Overall on speaking:**

- Walters, Lilly, Secrets of Successful Speakers.
- Berkun, Scott, Confessions of a Public Speaker.
- Gall, Carmine, The Presentation Secrets of Steve Jobs.

» **Resources on the internet**

- www.lars-sudmann.com
  Lars Sudmann's web page and blog on leadership and communication, including speaking videos from Lars' appearances at major speaking events.

- www.redphoenixagency.com
  Paul Arinaga's company for marketing communications, strategy and information design.

- www.mannerofspeaking.org
  The blog of our friend John Zimmer. John is a champion speaker and regularly shares his thoughts on public speaking, as well as speech analyses and great quotes for public speakers.

BEFORE BECOMING A SMARTPRESENTER:

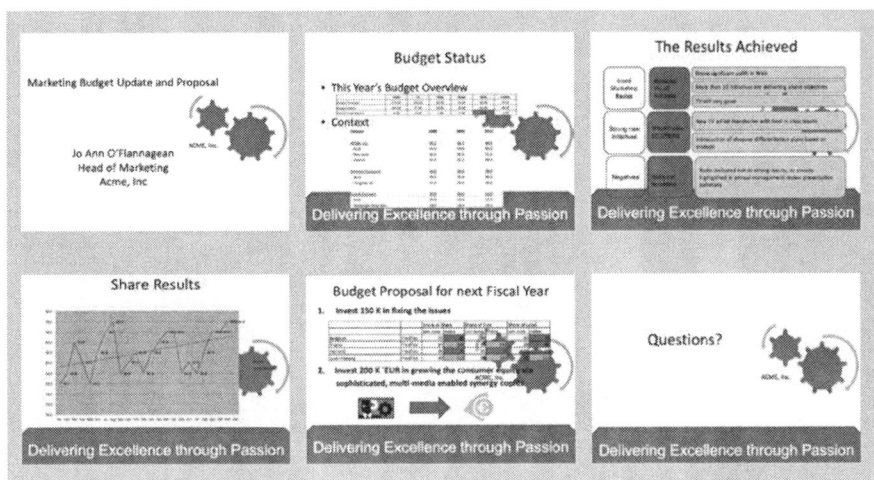

AFTER BECOMING A SMARTPRESENTER:

Acknowledgements

The SmartPresenter was a lengthy "labor of love" which wouldn't have been possible without the support of the following people. We'd like to thank our partners Veronica Hertling-Schwietzke and Dr. Katharina Baumgarten, both high-powered businesswomen who frequently give presentations, for providing invaluable feedback from the "trenches" and for keeping us going.

Several Toastmasters clubs in the Belgian area provided us with the opportunity to test and refine our ideas for this book. These are the Brussels Toastmasters Club (of which we are both long-time members and past club officers) the Leuven Toastmasters Club, the Ghent Toastmasters Club, the Atomium Toastmasters Club and the Hasselt Toastmasters Club. Thank you also to The Toastmasters Poland Leadership Institute where Lars presented The SmartPresenter concept.

We'd also like to thank Chalks Corriette, President of People To People International, and the Hub Brussels for inviting us to present the POINT formula during workshops and at other gatherings. The feedback we gathered from participants was invaluable in improving this book.

Modern collaboration tools such as Skype for video conferencing, Google Docs for real-time collaboration and Dropbox for document sharing were also helpful, as was istockphoto.com for the pictures.

We'd like to express our very special thanks to Jo Ann Broger and Tom Aerden. Tom provided very useful feedback from his perspective as a seasoned technology marketer and presenter. Jo Ann, who is former director of the American Chamber of Commerce in Belgium, provided extensive feedback based on her lengthy international business career, understanding of North American business culture and perspective as a senior female executive.

ACKNOWLEDGEMENTS

Index

8
80/20 Rule, 5

A
Action verbs, 58
Audience
　　Demographics, Psychographics, Learning style, Cognitive type, 21

B
Black screen, 108
Blackout, 128
Bullets, 56, 57, 60, 88, 96, 97, 111, 162
　　Beyond bullets, 60, 85, 88
　　Powerful visual, 61,75
　　Quotation or testimonial, 48, 61, 74, 88, 141, 162
　　Real or stylized example, 60, 73, 88, 141
　　Schematic or conceptual framework, 60, 62, 88
　　Step-wise approach, 40, 60, 61, 88, 141, 162
　　Tell a story, 43,48, 61, 80, 88

C
Call to action, 19, 20, 43, 44, 51
Chart styles, 99
Charts, 60, 63, 66, 67, 69, 70, 71, 73, 85, 100, 113, 119, 166, 169
Close, 46, 50, 51, 81, 120, 167

Closing, 46, 50, 51
Cognitive type
　　Analytical, Imaginative, Sequential, Interpersonal, 22
Corporate design, 115

D
Decision making unit (DMU), 23
Delivery
　　Audience lover, 125, 126
　　Blackout, 128, 133
　　Eye contact, 130
　　Fidgeting, 130, 132
　　Hands, 131, 132
　　Movement, 131
　　Presentation style, 129
　　Remote control device, 108, 128, 133
　　Screen lover, 126, 127
　　Stage fright, 130
　　Tennis spectator, 126, 127
　　Timing, 129

E
Efficiency, 3,4,5
Emotional connection, 127
Eye contact, 130

F
Fidgeting, 130, 132
Five minute challenge, 112

Lightning Source UK Ltd.
Milton Keynes UK
UKOW05n0629270614

234136UK00001B/5/P